"With the evolution of the B2B buying experience becoming more digital, group-led, and personalized, centering around the customer experience is critical. In *The CX Imperative*, Fithian and Rosenberg offer a much-needed roadmap to help companies adopt a pervasive CX mindset that avoids the Great Distancing and, instead, drives improved customer and corporate value."

Etosha Thurman, CMO, SAP Intelligent Spend & Business Network

"Many organizations don't realize how far they've strayed from their customers—until it's too late. *The CX Imperative* is a wake-up call, providing a sharp, well-structured approach to bridging that gap and making customer connection a business-wide priority. Fithian and Rosenberg show how to make CX work at scale."

Jeanne Bliss, pioneering chief customer officer, bestselling author, and founder of Customer Bliss

"For CX to truly matter, it can't live on the sidelines—it must be embedded into the DNA of the organization. *The CX Imperative* delivers a sharp, structured approach to making that a reality."

Vinny Rinaldi, vice president, media & marketing technology, The Hershey Company

"This is a must-read book for practitioners who are tasked with making CX front and center for businesses. With an approach that encourages both data-driven insights and a deep dive into actual customer experiences and the culture that drives them, *The CX Imperative* lays out an impressive blueprint for any twenty-first-century brand that wants to return to putting customers first."

P. V. Kannan, CEO, [24]7.ai, and author of *The Age of Intent*

amplify

an imprint of Amplify | Publishing Group

www.amplifypublishinggroup.com

The CX Imperative: Five Strategic Practices for Renewal of the Customer-Centered Enterprise

For more information, please contact:
Amplify Publishing, an imprint of Amplify Publishing Group
620 Herndon Parkway, Suite 220
Herndon, VA 20170
info@amplifypublishing.com

Library of Congress Control Number: 2025902310

CPSIA Code: PRV0425A

ISBN-13: 979-8-89138-581-8

Printed in the United States

THE
CX
IMPERATIVE

Five Strategic Practices
for Renewal of the
Customer-Centered Enterprise

Mark Fithian   Jeff Rosenberg

amplify
an imprint of Amplify Publishing Group

CONTENTS

OUR THESIS

We're excited to put our perspective into the customer experience (CX) universe, having spent our careers working for and consulting with large global enterprises on all things CX.

To orient you to our perspective at a high level prior to getting into the details, we thought it would be helpful (and expedient) to provide a snapshot of this book's core premise. We hope you enjoy and get a lot out of the concepts we lay out.

PROBLEM

Customers value the holistic experience they have with companies. It drives decision-making (to become a customer, to remain a customer).

Companies are generally not set up to deliver experiences well in perpetuity and at scale. Traditional operational silos coupled with the immaturity of CX as a discipline result in a fractured experience.

CAUSE

Shareholder primacy, which causes corporations to be run more like financial instruments than engines of customer value delivery, leads to misfocused management.

As corporate structures have evolved with the rise of the megacompany, there has been a Great Distancing from the customer.

SOLUTION

We need to challenge conventional wisdom, challenge the status quo, reinstate some practices that existed before shareholder primacy took over in the mid-1900s, and embed customer centricity in the DNA of the organization through the five dimensions of CX excellence we've identified in our client work:

- Insights
- Strategy
- Blueprints
- Operating Model
- Culture

INTRODUCTION

Organizations can no longer rely on traditional business practices—they are simply ill-suited for the unprecedented complexity in today's business environment.

▶ The factors that drive customer choice and loyalty are evolving. Today, customers increasingly value the entirety of their experience—encompassing product performance, services, and every interaction—not just at a single moment but consistently over time.

▶ The business environment is in a perpetual state of change. Customer expectations are shifting rapidly. Technology advancements are creating unforeseen marketspaces. Competitors seemingly come out of nowhere and disrupt once-predictable markets. Employees have evolving expectations of their employers and are harder to retain.

▶ Companies are struggling to coordinate and align customer experience execution across functions. They don't know the best work to be done. Companies are typically siloed and fractured, with teams isolated from one another's activities and from one another.

▶ Teams are also isolated in many ways from the customers they serve. We believe this is caused by what we call the Great Distancing: the straying of the corporation away from the customer philosophically (by overemphasizing shareholder primacy) and practically (by not knowing customers deeply as humans).

The challenges are palpable. Meeting after meeting, year after year, we all see the difficulty of getting things done, of working in and running large organizations. How can organizations break out of this cycle of being buried under increasing complexity? How can they clear away the noise and focus on what matters most? Our perspective is that a focus on the customer and the entirety of the customer experience is the way to create clarity, grow, become more efficient, and be better corporate stewards.

Our perspective is that customer experience must become a core traditional business practice.

Customer experience. CX. A term, a label, a function, a discipline, a practice. CX has grown in prominence over the past several decades from a natural extension of the customer service revolution in the '80s, to customer relationship management in the '90s, and then into digital experience since the rise of the internet. CX is a hot topic. All you have to do is look at the number of CX-related positions in companies over the past several years to know that CX has taken off. CX work is now beginning to formalize, particularly around experience mapping, blueprinting, and service design.

We'd like to offer a perspective on CX from a different angle, which is how companies can adopt a permanent, pervasive CX mindset that alters the inner workings of the organization without a big transformation effort. Companies can become innately CX focused across the organization, not just at the edges where experiences are designed and executed.

Why take this broad, strategic view of CX? Because CX is important work—in many cases existential—to all stakeholders:

▸ Customers who benefit from higher-value experiences
▸ Employees who have a greater sense of purpose and meaning in their work
▸ Companies who generate greater economic returns over time
▸ Shareholders who realize improved growth in their investment

Despite these proven benefits, there are structural forces working against adoption of mindsets and practices that lead to what we refer to as Strategic CX—a holistic, company-wide perspective on customer experience. The following are some of the forces that stand in the way of Strategic CX:

▸ The corporation is engineered to primarily serve shareholders, not customers.
▸ Process execution is generally seen as the end, not the means.
▸ Customer experience is often seen as a softer, dispensable component of the customer lifecycle; it is not inclusive

of the product experience and not a driver of tangible business value.

▸ CX can be a longer-term play, which is at odds with a "this quarter" mentality.

Here's where we can make things a little easier on everyone involved: You are already doing CX work. You are already spending billions every year on customer experience. Products, services, emails, sales calls, marketing campaigns, events, brand work, retail environments, websites, mobile apps—the money is being spent. The question is this: Are organizations willing to be courageous in leading an effort to align, connect, and integrate this work? If so, how can organizations do what they are doing today in a better, more coordinated way?

We offer this book as part of a Strategic CX movement. We are sharing our perspective on an enterprise-wide approach to CX as well as the methodologies and frameworks that help facilitate our work with clients. We want to do whatever we can to accelerate the transformation from shareholder-based decision-making to customer-based decision-making.

How This Book Is Organized

We begin with some important context setting to provide the *why* behind CX:

Chapter 1: **REVOLUTION**	Premise for our point of view—that the modern corporation has distanced itself from the customers it serves
Chapter 2: **THE CASE FOR CX**	Benefits associated with CX for customers, employees, and the corporate entity
Chapter 3: **ASSESSMENT**	How to take stock of where your company is with CX

CX requires total enterprise involvement and a broad strategic perspective. The framework we use to achieve this consists of five key components:

Chapter 4: **INSIGHTS**	Specific type of customer insights required to drive CX efforts
Chapter 5: **STRATEGY**	Focused approach to coordinating and aligning action
Chapter 6: **BLUEPRINTS**	Purposeful and intentional experience design
Chapter 7: **OPERATING MODEL**	How teams work together to achieve CX at scale
Chapter 8: **CULTURE**	How the organization thinks about and embraces CX

Who This Book Is For

We have encountered countless people who truly want to do what's right for the customer, people who are disheartened that they work in organizations that know for a fact they are producing frustrating experiences for customers but can't do the necessary work to pull out of that tailspin. Similarly, we've seen a lot of people who see CX as an opportunity to enhance company performance, people who see value left on the table day in and day out. These include frontline people, functional workers, leaders, and executives.

Some people just get it. This book is for you.

We've met countless people who have to be convinced that the customer experience matters enough to take action. They see little to no value in focusing on customer experience, expending effort on it, or investing money in it. This book is *not* for them. We are not here to convince the skeptics. We are here to support, bolster, and accelerate the work of CX Champions.

CX Champions can exist anywhere in the organization—product, sales, marketing, brand, customer service, finance, HR, or operations. Champions have many different titles. They could run large teams or be sole practitioners. They work on small fixes and large transformations. They have many success stories and many failures. They are avid teachers, influencers, and conveners. They believe deeply in CX and desperately want their organizations to be better, more intentional experience-driven companies. And they see themselves as the agents of change to make this happen.

What You Will Get Out of It

Think of this book as a new natural way of working. Without the heavy lift of culture change or transformation, you'll get a holistic framework for thinking expansively about how to embed CX mindsets, sensibilities, and practices into the DNA of your organization. CX is not a presentation layer pursuit. Rather, it requires enterprise-wide participation. As we lay out in this book, it's not about adding CX as a dimension across the organization but rather reconstituting the way teams consider, plan, and execute in alignment with one another in service of the customer.

The perspective we share is distilled from years of working with all levels of clients spanning multiple industries across the world. We have been shoulder to shoulder with our clients, working across the spectrum of Strategic CX components. Here, we share a synthesized set of tools and frameworks we use with clients to drive their businesses forward. This book is about what needs to be thought through to get to permanent CX at scale; it does not provide definitive answers that can be lifted and applied uniformly since this work is highly specialized to the unique attributes of companies and their customers.

Why We Wrote This

WideOpen, our Strategic CX consultancy, believes in customer centricity and CX as central to the evolution of the corporation. We believe in CX, and we believe in CX Champions. We believe CX can solve many of the challenges and frustrations that CX Champions face as they valiantly attempt to carry the banner of CX in their organizations, working hard to ward off opposition, entrenched habits, cultural norms, and apathy.

We have been strong advocates for Strategic CX on behalf of our clients for many years, learning and doing alongside them, seeing what works and what doesn't. We've developed numerous methods and frameworks over this time span and decided it was time to turn WideOpen inside out and share our insights with the CX community. Our efforts are largely an altruistic endeavor; we would like to see companies begin to embrace CX as a new way of operating, and the more we can put thinking into the world that delivers improvement, the better off we all are—in both our professional and personal lives.

For companies to thrive at scale in perpetuity, there has to be a focus and emphasis on the customer, on customer experience. We believe it is not the default proposition of the modern corporation to have such a customer-centric mindset and approach and that companies need to force a pendulum swing back to certain premodern mindsets and practices. To achieve this over time and at scale, companies need to focus on customer experience, both front stage (what the customer sees) and backstage (how the organization delivers experiences).

As we'll lay out in chapter 1, the modern corporation is simply not set up to be customer centric.

1

REVOLUTION

*The Straying of the
Modern Corporation*

Think of a great single experience you've had with a company. Perhaps the product was incredible, a person helping you was amazing, or a process worked flawlessly. Maybe you had an issue with the product and customer service resolved it above and beyond your expectations. Was the retail environment easy to navigate and enjoyable? Maybe there was a program made available to you that helped you learn how to use a product properly.

Now think of a great relationship you've had with a company over time, where you generally love their products or you enjoy dealing with them. Maybe you love the range of products they offer. Do you like how easy it is to purchase from them? Or possibly you like how they help you navigate to the right product or service.

Now think about a company where the total customer experience—all facets of your interactions with them—is running on all cylinders consistently, without fail, and over a long period of time, no matter what the product is or who you are dealing with at the company. The way you find products, the products themselves, ancillary products, support services, people, physical environments, websites, and mobile apps work together seamlessly. Everything is integrated and frictionless.

Thinking of a great single experience is easy. Thinking of a great relationship becomes a bit more difficult. Thinking of a great total customer experience (consistently and over time) is near impossible. Love Apple products? Sure. How about working with iTunes? Not so much. Love the Disney theme park experience? Definitely. But trying to figure out the latest version of Lightning Lane? A tough task.

We believe in a future where companies are innately aware of, thinking about, and executing great total customer experiences as a matter of course, as part of their DNA and woven into the fabric of the corporation. But think about it: Why isn't it that way already?

The Great Distancing

There is a fundamental flaw in the operating model of the modern corporation: It is largely based on the inertia of how corporations have evolved since the rise of the megacompany. It takes as given the structures and processes of the corporations that have come before them—how companies are organized, common processes, traditional practices—except they have accentuated the weaknesses and abandoned the strengths.

The core issue at hand is that companies tend to look inward and manage as if managing the company was the job instead of managing to build value for customers. Instead of leaning full throttle into their customers to deliver unmatched value on a continuous basis, companies go about their daily routines, executing processes and functions detached from customers. This results in misfocused management, whereby companies run a campaign, create an event, or develop a product based on heads-down inertia as opposed to thinking critically about the markets they serve and what customers need and expect from the company.

There is no disputing the success of companies generally. You can't argue with companies that have grown from nothing to multimillion- and multibillion-dollar companies. We are not attacking any particular company. We are instead challenging blind acceptance of the theories, practices, habits, and conventional wisdom that have evolved unquestioned over the past decades.

Companies need to rethink their approach to business practices. The business world is too unstable and unpredictable. Technology and globalization ushered in a wave of continuous and accelerated change that makes it challenging to make the thousands of business decisions necessary to run a company on any given day. You likely experience it all the time. The answers to "what product features should we prioritize," "what content should we create," "what's our messaging," and "how can we foster loyalty" are elusive. The Great Distancing—the straying of the corporation away from the customer and toward misfocused management—has made this even more challenging.

THE DANGER OF DISTANCING

Irrelevance

Blockbuster is a great example of a company that lost mightily because it was driven (in part) by hubris, not customer centricity. It ignored a seismic market shift. AOL and Kodak did the same. Those two companies survived but as shadows of their former selves.

Missed Opportunity

Pre-cloud, many (if not all) of the large, traditional enterprise technology vendors were intensely sales oriented, aggressively selling software to companies whether they needed the software or not. And once that software was sold, the relationship was managed for additional sales, not for successful adoption of the software.

Enter the cloud and new born-on-the-cloud entrants, and the traditional players saw their market share erode and their sales flatten, losing to these new entrants. The traditional players eventually adapted but at a mighty opportunity cost.

Annoyed Customers

Even if a company doesn't lose market share or revenue, not being attuned to customer needs causes unnecessary drag on the system: both customers and employees are frustrated. Time and effort has to be spent on reworking, making things right, and dealing with general unhappiness in the system. Employees aren't confident in decision-making. Customers have fewer reasons to remain loyal.

How We Got Here

It hasn't always been this way. Prior to the evolution of the modern corporation and before overwrought corporate structures took root, businesses were close to the customers they served. They knew customers intimately. Let's go way back for a minute. Picture a business before the 1700s. Employees in all companies likely at least saw the retail or wholesale customers they were serving. Most actually interacted with customers. Many knew customers by name.

Then the industrial revolution hit in the late 1700s, more formal corporate structures began to arise, and the Great Distancing began. In the 1800s, corporations, once chartered by governments as mechanisms to facilitate trade and provide social benefit, were allowed to privatize, and the trajectory of the corporation was altered forever, eventually leading to serving the shareholder (with corporate profits) as the primary stakeholder. That continues to this day.

Over time, as companies got larger and more geographically dispersed, even more sophisticated management structures took shape. Companies got bigger, new corporate functions began to mature, and more management layers were introduced. Companies began to look inward, and any looks outward were typically directed at competitors. Maximizing shareholder value overtook maximizing stakeholder value as the primary goal of the corporation—an unquestioned, steadfast focus among corporate managers. *Dodge v. Ford Motor Co.* in 1919 solidified this with the court's decision that forced Ford to operate in the interests of its shareholders rather than the interests of customers or its employees.

Management theories taken as granted and taught in business schools reinforced managements' distance from customers. Finance and accounting mindsets drove corporate decision-making. CEOs typically rose out of the finance and accounting ranks.

Today, companies are even more complex (structures, policies, functions, regulatory requirements), and the world of business is more complex (technology, data, converging marketspaces). Companies are continuously seeking ways to increase sales, reduce costs, beat the competition, and remain relevant. Employees come and go with increasing frequency. Customers are in control. The game is changing; organizations no longer can rely on historical practices to carry them forward.

Management theories of the mid-1900s are not adapted for today's environment. There are no natural engrained cross-functional practices around the customer or customer experience. Management theories do not establish the customer as the key dynamic. Further, management theories do not instill customer management as a key competency.

Large companies are organized into functional silos based on historical and structural factors that emphasize specialization and efficiency. This structure aligns to the prevailing corporate management theories of hierarchy and functional accountability. Teams charged with customer experience work (typically sales, marketing, digital, customer support, customer success, training, and others) are doing the best they can but within their functional silos and without an apparatus in place to coordinate, align, and connect experience execution—across teams and to the customer.

Revolution

Indeed, CX is on an upward trajectory. It's getting more attention than ever. But the hard work of CX isn't happening fast enough or broadly enough across (and within) organizations. It's not that anyone is at fault necessarily. It's that customer centricity is not the default way of operating due to the Great Distancing. The business community can achieve customer centricity as the norm but not without a concerted cross-discipline, multidimensional movement.

What we all want as CX Champions is a pivot to customer centricity. It benefits everyone, including:

▶ Customers, who demand better experiences. (All the data shows customers value experience, and that it factors heavily in their decision to become a customer and remain a customer.)

▶ Employees, who increasingly value purpose in their jobs and want to do right by the customer. (We continuously hear clients talk about issues the organization has and how they result in bad customer experiences.)

▶ The corporate entity, which is always seeking new growth avenues. (Studies show that focusing on CX improves performance; see next chapter.)

This is the potential of CX. A better ecosystem of value delivery and value creation, both financial and nonfinancial. CX is mission critical, and organizations need to coordinate and align efforts in service of the customer.

We are calling for a CX revolution. We want to bring about an awareness and awakening that recognizes things do not need to be this way. Organizations can do better. Better for customers, better for employees, better for the company. They can do this by keeping their eyes on the main unit (the customer), not the misfocused unit (internal functions).

There are pockets of progress, and they are expanding. Within companies, there are increasing numbers of CX Champions who believe in CX and are making the case internally. The commonly held belief that the corporation exists to maximize shareholder value is now up for debate, even among business leaders. Consider these instances:

- ▶ Starbucks CEO Howard Shultz said, "The company must shift its focus away from bureaucracy and back to customers. We need to reignite the emotional attachment with our customers."
- ▶ Fred Reicheld, creator of the Net Promoter system, believes, "The primary purpose of an organization isn't shareholder returns but rather to enrich the lives of its customers."
- ▶ Business Roundtable in 2019 issued their periodic "Statement on the Purpose of a Corporation," which was signed by 181 CEOs committing to lead their companies for the benefit of all stakeholders—customers, employees, suppliers, communities, and shareholders. In prior years, this statement of purpose only endorsed shareholder primacy.

These examples challenging conventional wisdom remind us that you don't have to take as granted the practices we have all learned and followed in the past. Norms are being questioned and challenged every day throughout our lives. What was once a given can no longer be counted on. Conventional wisdom is only conventional in our lifetimes. We learn the theories of our time. But theories come and go and get replaced by other theories.

Given the increased complexities of business today, now more than ever organizations need to weave the customer into their operating models and keep the customer permanently embedded.

To make this take hold broadly, we all need to bring about a customer centricity revolution. Companies need to understand the opportunity—to believe in it to their core— that becoming customer centric is vital to their ongoing success and longevity. CX is not a project or better relationship management or better service. It is reformation of the corporate entity to orchestrate and synchronize all of its efforts with the customer in mind.

We posit that the notion of the corporate entity can be reformulated and that CX Champions and the larger CX community can help foster the pivot from shareholder value to customer value, from shareholder primacy to customer primacy. Together we can reconstitute the modern corporation. It's the right thing to do, yes, but the complexity of operating in today's global business environment also demands change.

Key Points Recap

▶ Organizations don't have to accept the decades-old business practices taught in business schools and workplaces as given or mandated.

▶ Corporations that exclusively focus on shareholder value do so at their own risk; they may not see the long-term value of CX and/or may sacrifice it for short-term performance.

▶ Given the increasing complexity of operating in today's business environment, companies need to get the customer back into the DNA of the company.

You already understand the value of focusing on customer experience. Let's expand the tent and bring others along to our way of thinking. That starts with making a well-rounded case for CX that covers a range of internal company interests, which we address next in chapter 2.

CHAPTER 2 OVERVIEW

TOPIC PREVIEW	▸ Our definition of CX encompasses the totality of everything the customers sees, touches, does, or feels—including the product.
	▸ CX impacts business metrics and therefore needs to be positioned as mission critical.
	▸ A focus on CX can positively impact customers, employees, and the company.
What we mean by **THE CASE FOR CX**	Often, companies need to develop business cases to receive approval for key initiatives that require investment. This is true for CX initiatives as well, but companies need to go further and make a case for why CX is important and worthy of time, attention, and budget.
Why **THE CASE FOR CHANGE** *is important*	It specifies and formalizes how the company should think about the range of benefits a focus on CX can achieve.
With **THE CASE FOR CHANGE...**	CX will be widely understood to be—and positioned as—mission critical to the business, to growth, and to ongoing viability.
Without **THE CASE FOR CHANGE...**	CX will be seen as a presentation layer, extraneous, a nice-to-have.

2

THE CASE FOR CX

*Linking Customer Experience
to Business Metrics*

Most people in most companies either aren't aware of the benefits of CX or they ignore CX because they think it's not core to the business. We in the CX community cannot allow this perception to perpetuate. Study after study has shown that companies that successfully focus on and invest in customer experience improve their performance as a result. They outpace their peers in terms of revenue growth and cost efficiencies and generally improve the health of their business. Customer experience work is not about soft measures. It's high-impact, mission-critical work that moves metrics that matter. Consider this:

According to McKinsey & Co., companies that prioritize customer experience outperform their competitors, with a 2.4 times increase in revenue growth compared to companies that do not prioritize CX.

Why isn't every company clamoring to get their CX machinery up and running?

Unlike other corporate functions (product, manufacturing, finance, marketing, human resources, etc.), customer experience as a practice—as a discipline—is still in its infancy. Born out of customer service, marketing (demand generation/customer relationship marketing), digital (user experience design), customer satisfaction (e.g., customer satisfaction [CSAT]), and net promoter score (NPS), CX has evolved into its own set of beliefs and practices. However, it's still not a mature core competency practice. It lacks a unified definition, it's broad and all encompassing, it's difficult to measure holistically, and it's challenging to coalesce action. It's often misunderstood or perceived by executives as expensive or expendable.

CX is often viewed as soft, subjective, intangible, difficult to quantify, and a cost center. Leadership often thinks of CX as something managed off to the side, adjacent to the product, the responsibility of no one. That diminishes the strategic value of CX.

We look at CX more expansively, strategically, and existentially—as the entirety of the business itself. *Customer experience is the customer*, which is the reason the company exists in the first place. CX is not a department, although it may be managed through a department. It's not confined to frontline experiences such as customer service, retail, or websites. CX needs to be the DNA of the organization, not fit into the organization but inextricably inseparable from any part of the business.

CX is the business.

We define customer experience as:

CX = Products + Interactions + Engagement + Relationship

It's anything the customer sees, touches, does, or feels with the company. Therefore, all functions—product, sales, marketing, operations, finance, human resources, C-suite—play a role in delivering value to customers, either directly or indirectly.

Leveling Up CX Impact

When trying to effect change in a running organization that is already overloaded with activity, priorities, needs, and budget requests, CX Champions have to convince leadership and their peers that CX is a worthwhile pursuit. They have to make a case for change on an ongoing basis. They have to continuously cheerlead. But to do that, you must first get leadership on board. And one of the best ways to get leadership on board is by showing them that CX impacts real business metrics.

If CX is the business, it follows logically that CX metrics are business metrics. This means you don't need to invent or install a new metrics system in the business to track CX success. You can use metrics that are already in place: revenue, costs, margin, profit, etc. This is not hyperbole. Studies by McKinsey, Forrester, and other consultancies have tracked at this altitude, demonstrating, for instance, the impact on shareholder value of a company being a CX leader vs. a CX laggard.

Often, companies think of CX as presentation layer activities (what the customer sees), so they think of metrics like email open rates, online conversion, customer satisfaction, and NPS. Those metrics certainly are affected. But we think in terms of revenue, growth, and cost reduction. CX rises to board-level metrics.

CX is essential to how an organization delivers and captures value, with due recognition given to the fact that organizations generate other income through financial instrumentation and other means.

The Benefits of CX

A great customer experience can fuel a flywheel that delivers improved performance and efficiency. When making the case for CX, organizations need to be thinking about the full range of benefits and impact to customers, to employees, and to the company, as shown in Table 2.1.

CUSTOMER	EMPLOYEES	COMPANY
▸ Success with the product	▸ Greater sense of purpose	▸ Differentiation
▸ Avoidance of frustration and friction	▸ Sense of accomplishment	▸ Expanded opportunities for value delivery
▸ Sense of confidence/ empowerment	▸ Sense of being supported by the organization	▸ Product-market fit
		▸ Increased revenue and growth
		▸ Improved operational efficiency

CUSTOMER	EMPLOYEES	COMPANY
▸ Expectations met ▸ Greater ROI on purchase	▸ Reduction in dealing with frustrated customers ▸ Reduction in barriers to goal achievement	▸ Sustained market relevance ▸ Customer advocacy ▸ Improved customer retention ▸ Improved employee retention

Table 2.1: Representative Positive CX Impact

Making the Case: Seeking Resources

To deliver on the potential of embedding a CX mindset in the organization, CX Practitioners—the many teams across the organization charged with executing CX—need resources: people, time, and budget. As we mentioned previously, the good news is that you are already doing CX. Your company has invested billions of dollars in CX. Your company does CX every day. All companies currently execute customer experience across product, sales, marketing, digital, service, and support. You simply can't have a business without customer experience; it's inherent. At the very minimum, there is value in examining those efforts and aligning them for more efficient execution and better CX outcomes.

Typically we see a progression over time, starting with needing permission to explore opportunities for CX impact, to time and budget to plan and scope, to time and budget to execute. These are the three tiers of making the case for change (persuading organizational teams and executives to move from CX apathy/negative to CX neutral/positive), as depicted in Table 2.2:

TIER	LABEL	DESCRIPTION	LEADERSHIP ASK
Tier I	Generic CX Impact	Ties CX work to top-level metrics. Intended to create awareness of CX as a strategic imperative	Interest in CX
Tier II	General Business Impact	Connects CX value to the company based on company focus and priorities	Advocacy for CX
Tier III	Initiative ROI	Requests budget and resources to pursue CX efforts	Funding for CX

Table 2.2 The Case for Change Tiers

▶ For Tier I, CX Champions can leverage studies that show the impact of a company being a CX leader. McKinsey, Harvard Business Review, Forrester, PwC, and KPMG studies have shown the improved financial and stock market performance of CX leader companies.

▶ For Tier II, CX Champions can model the potential of CX improvements specifically for their company.

▶ For Tier III, CX Champions can build a precise business case to seek funding for a specific initiative.

The chapter on culture (chapter 8) covers some of the other means of winning hearts and minds among colleagues more specifically. The point here is to be bold in asserting the economic impact of becoming more customer centric.

IMPACT OF CUSTOMER EXPERIENCE WORK

Revenue Impact

- Customers who had the best past experiences spend 140% more compared to those who had poor experiences. (*Harvard Business Review*)
- Companies that prioritize customer experience outperform their competitors, with a 2.4 times increase in revenue growth compared to companies that do not prioritize CX. (McKinsey & Company)
- Companies effective at CX can realize a 15% increase in sales conversion. (McKinsey & Company)
- Companies with a customer experience mindset drive revenue 4–8% higher than the rest of their industries. (Bain & Company)
- Brands with superior customer experience bring in 5.7 times more revenue than competitors that lag in customer experience. (Forrester Research)

Cost Impact

- Companies effective at CX can realize a 30% lower cost-to-serve. (McKinsey & Company)
- Companies that use tools like customer journey maps reduce their cost of service by 15–20%. (McKinsey & Company)
- Offering a high-quality customer experience can lower the cost of serving customers by up to 33%. (Deloitte)

Secondary Impact Measures

- 73% of consumers say that a good experience is a key factor in influencing their brand loyalty. (PwC)
- 32% of consumers say they will walk away from a brand they love after just one bad experience; 59% will walk away after several bad experiences. (PwC)
- Companies effective at CX can realize a 20%improvement in customer satisfaction. (McKinsey & Company)
- Companies effective at CX can realize a 30% increase in employee engagement. (McKinsey & Company)
- 36% of top CX companies exceeded their top business goal by a significant margin, compared to only 12% of less customer-focused companies. (Adobe)
- Companies that lead in customer experience outperform laggards by nearly 80%. (Forrester Research)

Key Points Recap

▶ CX is the totality of all interactions, including product, and includes both rational and emotional states (what the customer sees, touches, does, and feels).

▶ Be bold in your assertion that CX can drive both business-level metrics (e.g., revenue, costs) and business alignment. It can eliminate overlaps in experience initiatives, close customer experience gaps, drive cross-functional communication and collaboration, and drive a more efficient operation overall.

▶ Factor employee satisfaction, engagement, and retention into the equation. CX heavily impacts those charged with executing CX by creating a more effective and impactful work environment.

Now that you have a better grasp of the strategic importance of CX, next we'll look at how to evaluate where the business stands on CX by conducting an assessment to reveal strengths and weaknesses.

CHAPTER 3 OVERVIEW

TOPIC PREVIEW

- ▶ An honest, transparent assessment of the current state of CX within a company is a great way to take stock of successes and failures and establish priorities for future improvements.

- ▶ An assessment can be administered both at the start of a formalized pursuit of CX as well as ongoing (e.g., annually).

- ▶ Our assessment framework establishes key criteria for evaluation.

What we mean by **ASSESSMENT**

A CX assessment is a subjective perspective on where the company rates itself on the critical areas of CX development.

Why **ASSESSMENT** *is important*

An assessment tracks improvement over time and identifies areas for improvement, but even more so, it fosters communication across functions to ensure teams are in alignment on the state of CX in the company.

With **ASSESSMENT...**

The company knows where it stands on the critical components of permanent CX at scale—a shared, cross-functional perspective.

Without **ASSESSMENT...**

Teams may have different perspectives on how well the company is doing, and the company doesn't know which critical gaps exist and should be prioritized for attention.

3

ASSESSMENT

Creating a Shared Awareness
of Current State CX

Achieving Clarity

As we have indicated, customer experience is an ongoing enterprise-wide endeavor. How can organizations know where they stand on their CX pursuits as a company? How can they know if they're making progress? There is a continuous, always-on flow of work to be done around planning, coordination, alignment, process design, policy setting, capability development, and other components required to achieve CX success at scale. Organizations need a formalized way to keep track of it all.

Achieving CX excellence requires the organization to be firing on multiple cylinders. You can't only have one team interested in CX; you need all relevant teams engaged. You can't just have teams engaged; you need leadership belief and advocacy. You can't just have people on board; you need great customer insights. Organizations also need a strategy for direction and alignment as well as great execution, data, and technology. The absence of any of these elements makes it exponentially more difficult and slows things down and creates frustration.

Through our work with clients on all topics CX, we have identified the most critical practices of CX at scale (Figure 3.1). This Strategic CX model serves as context for the various practices and their components and demonstrates that CX is more than just presentation layer activities.

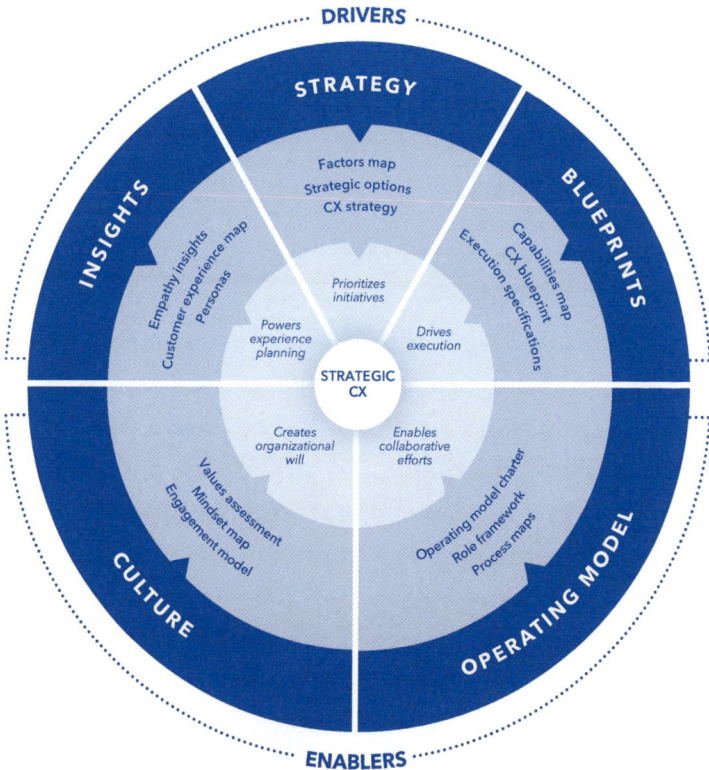

Figure 3.1: WideOpen's Strategic CX Model

When we begin working with clients who have just formed cross-functional CX committees (or some other form of cross-functional working relationships), we like to run the assessment as a clean starting point for establishing a baseline of where the organization is that day. This gives us a baseline that everyone contributes to and agrees on. We also like to run the assessment periodically to give time for CX teams to check in on how things are going as an organization.

We like to do assessments with clients in a formalized way based on predefined criteria. While we refer to this as a CX assessment, the intent is not to come out of it with a grade or score, nor is it necessarily to measure improvement year over year, although you could. The intent is to honor and celebrate the organization's successes and honestly reveal and acknowledge its weaknesses. The process shines a light on the reality of the state of CX and highlights areas of focus for coming efforts.

Our assessment tool (Figure 3.2 on pages 28–37) is also the conceptual model that we use to frame and contextualize CX efforts of all kinds. This means if a client hires us to work on one area of CX, we are always thinking about the other areas of CX to some extent. For us, it's inevitable. Say we're asked to develop a CX blueprint for a certain experience (for instance, the post-sale experience for an enterprise technology product). The blueprint we create—which will be developed from the customer back (more on that in the chapter on blueprinting)—will require new ways of working, either across functions or new processes, new policies, etc. This touches culture, the operating model, etc.

The assessment is designed to spark reflection and facilitate cross-functional dialogue. This straightforward model explores the five dimensions of CX excellence, which we elaborate on further in this book. At a foundational level, the assessment can serve as a catalyst for change, encouraging discussion and dialogue within the organization. Picture a meeting where the assessment is visible, either in a chart or on a wall. It allows for more focused, meaningful conversation and strategic planning. Are you working on the critical areas that will help the organization get better at CX? Why do you see this as a limitation? Where can you lean in for improvement?

Companies need to embrace the customer-centric practices necessary for sustained success: insights, strategic planning, blueprinting, operating model alignment, and cultural advocacy. Our assessment model follows this construct. Think of these practices as the critical enablers of CX at scale that the company should be pursuing, discussing, and improving upon. Subsequent chapters cover each component in more detail.

Assessment Tool

For each assessment criteria (the rows in Figure 3.2), CX teams can think critically and realistically about where the organization stands in the following terms:

► Characterization

    ▷ Current State: How the teams regard the current state, both positive and negative attributes. For instance, under Culture, the team may feel there isn't a general understanding of CX as critical to success, that leadership hasn't embraced CX as an area of focus for the company.

    ▷ Breadth/Depth: The extent to which the criteria is taking place across the organization being assessed (e.g., the entire organization, functional area, region). For example, under Insights, the organization may have great empathy insights but only for a specific customer segment, the purchase process, or Western Europe.

    ▷ Positive/Negative Aspects: Examples of what is working well and what isn't working so well. For instance, under Strategy, the team may say a strategy is in place, but certain teams don't know how to leverage it.

► Gaps: The nature of the gap between current state and desired future state. (If there is no defined or agreed upon future state, that's okay—teams can create early hypotheses on the desired future state.) For example, an organization may identify that there is a gap in governance but isn't ready to select a governance model. In this assessment, the team can simply note it as a critical gap.

Criteria	Question	Score
INSIGHTS		
Analysis	Are there deep human (empathy) insights?	0 1 2 3 4 5
Approach	Were insights derived qualitatively?	0 1 2 3 4 5
Artifacts	Is there a customer experience map?	0 1 2 3 4 5
	Are there customer personas?	0 1 2 3 4 5
	Are there role maps?	0 1 2 3 4 5
Attributes	Do insights include both emotional and rational data?	0 1 2 3 4 5
	Are there Lifeflow insights across the end-to-end lifecycle?	0 1 2 3 4 5
Activation	Are empathy insights being used to drive experience planning?	0 1 2 3 4 5

Characterization
Current State | Breadth/Depth | +/-Aspects

Gaps
Areas to Develop

Criteria	Question	Score
STRATEGY		
Analysis	Is there a clear perspective on the dynamics that impact our approach to CX?	0 1 2 3 4 5
Approach	Were strategic options explored and considered?	0 1 2 3 4 5
	Was the development approach inclusive?	0 1 2 3 4 5
Artifacts	Is there an organizational CX Strategy?	0 1 2 3 4 5
Attributes	Is there a vision that connects to action?	0 1 2 3 4 5
	Does the CXS reflect focused trade-offs?	0 1 2 3 4 5
	Is the CXS specific and understandable?	0 1 2 3 4 5
Activation	Is the CXS being used to prioritize experience efforts?	0 1 2 3 4 5

Characterization
Current State | Breadth/Depth | +/-Aspects

Gaps
Areas to Develop

Criteria	Question	Score
BLUEPRINTS		
Analysis	Is there a customer analysis?	0 1 2 3 4 5
	Is there a resource analysis?	0 1 2 3 4 5
	Is there a capabilities analysis?	0 1 2 3 4 5
Approach	Was the development approach inclusive?	0 1 2 3 4 5
	Did development follow a customer-back, intentional design process?	0 1 2 3 4 5
Artifacts	Is there a customer experience blueprint?	0 1 2 3 4 5
Attributes	Is the CEB longitudinal and omnichannel?	0 1 2 3 4 5
	Does the CEB specify and orchestrate execution?	0 1 2 3 4 5
Activation	Is the CEB used to drive execution?	0 1 2 3 4 5

Characterization
Current State | Breadth/Depth | +/-Aspects

Gaps
Areas to Develop

Criteria	Question	Score
OPERATING MODEL		
Analysis	Is there an operating model audit?	0 1 2 3 4 5
Approach	Was the process tailored to the organizational needs?	0 1 2 3 4 5
Artifacts	Is there a chartered operating model?	0 1 2 3 4 5
Attributes	Have roles and responsibilities been defined?	0 1 2 3 4 5
	Are standard processes and decision rights clear?	0 1 2 3 4 5
	Is it sanctioned by leadership?	0 1 2 3 4 5
	Is it lean and adaptive?	0 1 2 3 4 5
Activation	Is the operating model being used to improve collaboration?	0 1 2 3 4 5

Characterization
Current State | Breadth/Depth | +/-Aspects

Gaps
Areas to Develop

Criteria	Question	Score
CULTURE		
Analysis	Is there a values assessment?	0 1 2 3 4 5
	Is there mindset mapping?	0 1 2 3 4 5
Approach	Was the process inclusive?	0 1 2 3 4 5
Artifacts	Is there an engagement model?	0 1 2 3 4 5
Attributes	Is it inclusive of all audiences?	0 1 2 3 4 5
	Does it identify specific actions by audience segment?	0 1 2 3 4 5
Activation	Is the model being used to drive culture efforts?	0 1 2 3 4 5

Figure 3.2: CX Assessment Tool

Characterization
Current State | Breadth/Depth | +/-Aspects

Gaps
Areas to Develop

We have done these assessments several different ways. There is no right answer; it's a decision based on company culture and management style. Some lean more into quantitative data; others rely on attitudinal perspectives collected through conversations. Some seek more of an outside-in view, while others are capturing inside sentiment. Here are a few methods we've used:

- Individual stakeholder interviews: These are conducted by an unbiased individual partner, and stakeholders are asked about each of the assessment criteria. It is perhaps the most time-consuming approach but potentially the most valuable to understand *why*, increase stakeholder engagement, and enrich perspective on the model itself.
- Collaborative workshop: We love the assessment as a homework exercise for stakeholder workshops. It helps prepare the team to engage in the broad dimensionality of experience. Typically sent as a survey, the results are brought back in to the team workshop as a structured exercise to start a dialogue with the team around gaps and opportunities.
- Confidential survey: We like the survey method for efficiency and pure objectivity but find response levels to be challenging and lacking in insight versus other methods. When we do field a true survey, we'll tend to look at a specific area. Additional survey programming can be challenging given some of the context that respondents may need to understand the questions at face value.
- Expert assessment: Sometimes an objective third-party subject matter expert is brought in to conduct the

assessment through interviews, asset reviews, and expert evaluation. In this process, the expert will look for specific hallmarks (practices, policies, performance) and evidence to gauge maturity across the model.

Keep in mind the assessment can cover a single functional area or multiple functional areas. It's not reserved only for cross-functional, organization-wide CX efforts. It's still beneficial to conduct an assessment within a specific department or team.

We have seen this assessment leveraged by a single individual as they seek to garner support and generate enthusiasm around CX. The assessment ensures a holistic view on the current state, the gaps, and the work to be done. Being well versed in this well-rounded perspective on CX builds credibility and trust with peers and leadership. It's a great way to demonstrate command of all of the levers required to achieve Strategic CX at scale.

Once the assessment has been completed (either formally or informally), areas of attention will reveal themselves. Not all gaps need to be solved at once, but it is healthy to have a shared team-wide perspective on the work ahead and be intentional about how the team will approach addressing the identified areas of need.

We'll discuss each of these Strategic CX components along with our frameworks and methods to achieve success, having used them with clients over the years.

BEFORE & AFTER

Before Assessment: Unknown

A consumer packaged goods (CPG) client was attempting to improve the customer experience on several fronts in different areas of the business: digital, wholesale relationships, and certain retail businesses. Efforts were not only isolated, but the individual team members didn't know each other and weren't all aware of each other's efforts. Furthermore, each team had its own take on what was required to do CX work successfully as well as what capabilities the organization required. The practice of CX was in disarray; even more critically, the company didn't know where the issues were.

After Assessment: Clarity

We helped our CPG client harness its collective energy by forming a center of excellence and conducting a CX assessment. The assessment process not only revealed where things stood on the critical factors for CX success, but it also introduced cross-functional team members who might not ever have met if not for this process. The openness and transparency of the process created instant trust among the team, who were then able to agree on strengths and weaknesses and identify priorities for moving forward as an integrated unit.

Key Points Recap

▶ Run an assessment—not only as a marker of where you are today and to track progress over time but as a vehicle for cross-functional communication, collaboration, and relationship building.

▶ Be realistic and honest in the assessment process. There is nothing to be gained by trying to force an artificially high score.

▶ Embrace the deficiencies. That's where the potential wins are.

Now that you understand the role of the assessment, let's get into our methodologies around CX in practice, starting with the foundation, bedrock, and linchpin of CX at scale: deep human-centered insights about customers. That's the fuel that powers effective customer experience strategies.

CHAPTER 4 OVERVIEW

TOPIC PREVIEW

▶ Deep human insights about customers are required to determine the experiences needed to create to truly connect with customers.

▶ These empathy insights need to flow through the organization so everyone has and is looking at the same insights.

▶ Customer experience maps and personas are tools we find to be the most intuitive and effective at insights diffusion.

What we mean by **INSIGHTS**

Insights is a broad term that can apply to many different dimensions. When we talk about insights in the context of customer experience, we're referring to customer insights. And not all customer insights but specifically empathy insights—insights that paint a picture of the customers you're creating experiences for so you can visualize and identify with them.

Why **INSIGHTS** *are important*

Empathy insights are critical to reaching more deeply into the psyche of the customer to enable you to anticipate their needs, fulfill unmet and unspoken needs, and identify new territories for value delivery (and value creation). Without such insights, organizations cannot reach full potential and therefore leave financial value on the table.

With **INSIGHTS...**

You can picture in your mind's eye the humans for whom you are creating experiences. You have a well-rounded understanding of their needs, expectations, behaviors, and emotional states across the end-to-end experience.

Without **INSIGHTS...**

You can only go so far in your experience development efforts, focusing primarily on inertia (what has been done in the past) and on practices borrowed from other companies that may or may not connect with the unique intersection of a) what your customer needs b) from your company.

4

STRATEGIC PRACTICE ONE: INSIGHTS

Creating the Fuel Supply for CX Work

How do companies come out of nowhere to dominate a market? How do market leaders tumble toward obscurity? There are numerous factors that impact success (or lack thereof). One significant factor is the extent to which a company is highly attuned to the needs, expectations, and behaviors of their customers as well as adjacent customer segments.

In the case of companies on the rise, they identify and fulfill unmet customer needs.

In the case of companies on the decline, they have lost sight of what customers want and instead cling to managing in business-as-usual mode. This is the reality of the modern corporation. Even marketers, who are charged with connecting with customers, more often than not have never even met *one* of their company's customers. They certainly could not describe who their customers are in vivid detail.

Job number one of high-performance CX is continuously closing this customer intimacy gap at scale, making sure that all employees understand the customer and that they have the same shared understanding of the customer across teams. This is the hard but essential work of understanding customers deeply and diffusing that insight across the organization.

What do we mean by "insights"? Insights is a broad term that covers many types and facets, namely market, competitive, industry, and consumer insights. In our model for high-performance CX, we're concerned with *customer insights*—and not just any customer insights but *empathy insights*.

Empathy Insights Power CX

Empathy insights go beyond typical customer insights. Typical customer insights—which are also critically important—cover customer profile information (like age, gender, geographic region, etc.) and technographic information (like digital habits, devices, etc.). In B2B, typical customer insights will include job role and firmographics (e.g., company size, industry) plus other information like brand awareness, media consumption, etc. Empathy insights adds a very human layer on these standard data points.

Empathy insights represent the characteristics and attributes of customers that allow organizations to know their customers as people. They create a well-rounded, rich, full color, fully rendered view of the humans CX Practitioners create experiences for: their rational needs and expectations, their emotional needs and expectations. How they buy, how they use. Who they interact with along the experience— within the organization and within their own network. Which channels they use, when, and for which purpose. What the company is able to see (e.g., them coming to the company's website, talking with a salesperson) and what happens behind the curtain (e.g., customer discusses the decision with family, gets recommendations from friends).

Empathy insights uniquely allow CX Practitioners to see customers as humans, not just as data points. When you have real humans in mind, you can create more impactful experiences. It helps focus on the people on the other end of the experiences you're creating rather than on the experiences themselves.

When the customer is not the full focus of your efforts, riding alongside the entire way, CX Practitioners tend to focus on the content asset they're creating, the process for producing the customer experience, or the other range of internal factors versus the intersection of the customer and the experience itself. It is very, very easy—in fact, it's nearly always the default—to get sucked under the gravity of the internal processes and practices of the organization and focus internally rather than externally. When you are in a meeting with colleagues, the natural tendency is to talk about how the work will get done, how to navigate internal politics, or which metric to focus on. All of that needs to be discussed, but it's often at the expense of discussing the customer, what she wants in the moment, and how you can help *her* accomplish *her* tasks and hit on the right emotions.

Empathy is the most modern, advanced, and accurate way of describing the type of insights companies need as well as describing what teams need to have for their customers. It's often misunderstood and confused with sympathy. Sympathy is generally understood as feeling pity for someone's misfortune. Empathy is the ability to understand the feelings of another person.

For example, if you are building a profile of a business buyer of enterprise technology, empathy insights will include details like the following:

▸ They are buying software for thousands of end users, so if things go wrong, their job and reputation will be impacted. You need to understand that underpinning the normal buying process and associated tasks is the fact they are nervous about making the right choice.

▸ As they make their decision, they are seeking perspectives from end users, advice from IT, support from procurement, and permission from executives.

▸ They like to see the product in action to see how it looks and feels, above and beyond its functional capabilities.

▸ During implementation, there is a sense of helplessness as they have turned over control to technical implementers.

▸ They have great hope and anticipation during the testing and training phase of the customer experience—hope and anticipation for better workflow execution and for technology that teams like using every day.

Armed with these empathy insights, CX Practitioners can identify and lean into all sorts of artfully-designed experiences that reinforce positive attributes and allay, disarm, or solve negative attributes. Just think of the creativity that would come out of a workshop focused on creating interactions that helped address the feeling of helplessness and loss of control and visibility during technical implementation.

Organizations need to know customers intimately on a continuous basis. In the absence of relevant insights, companies risk straying from their customers and vice versa (customer needs evolve away from what the company provides). You don't want to miss big—and small—shifts in customer needs and expectations. It's not enough to know customer demographic data or transactional data. Organizations need to know them as people, as humans. What does that mean? Often those charged with customer experience-related work take an object-view of customers (not with bad intentions). Customers become units that receive the company's offering, content, or interactions. They are a silhouetted abstract mass of beings, not real people in the real world with real problems to solve. A famous film and television writer once said that he can't write scripts for millions of people. He has to picture one person receiving the content he's creating (in his case, it's his uncle). When CX Practitioners can picture a real person with real needs, thoughts, and feelings, they can be more purposeful and resonant in their CX work.

Customer insights are the lifeblood of sustained, scalable, high-performing CX efforts. More often than not, CX Practitioners have to make decisions with very little to go on and without an understanding of the humans they are creating experiences for. As mentioned in the Revolution chapter, it's simply the reality of the modern organization that has drifted away from customer intimacy and into managing at a distance in the abstract.

Insights is data, information, and knowledge, whereas empathy insights is being highly attuned to another's needs and feelings. It allows for *perspective taking*, allowing you to put yourself in the shoes of your customers. And empathy insights paint a full picture of your customers, which crucially includes emotional factors. Studies consistently show that emotional factors are more important to decision-making across the customer experience than rational ones (and believe it or not, emotions are even more important in B2B than in B2C). Emotions often play an outsized role across the customer lifecycle, influencing customer behavior, perceptions, satisfaction, and preference. Understanding and managing emotions effectively can lead to enhanced customer experiences and long-term loyalty.

- ▶ Prior to the purchase, making an emotional connection can capture the attention of potential customers. This can lead to trust and confidence; not surprisingly, customers are more likely to choose a product or service when they feel a sense of trust and confidence in the brand.
- ▶ Post purchase, the emotional experience significantly influences customer satisfaction. Positive emotions post purchase contribute to customer loyalty, whereas negative emotions can arise if expectations are not met. Building an emotional connection with customers fosters loyalty. Brands that understand and resonate with their customers' emotions can create strong bonds; customers

who have positive emotional experiences are more likely to become advocates for the brand.

Getting Great Empathy Insights

Practices around gathering competitive insights, industry insights, and market insights are typically well-covered through existing corporate practices; they are routine and mature. The type of insights that typically aren't available to CX Practitioners are empathy insights: insights about customers themselves, including what they do and how they think. Competitive insights can also be gleaned from customers of competitive products. Seeing the world through the eyes of the customer opens a world of possibilities.

To achieve the degree of customer centricity required to execute CX with excellence requires CX practitioners to be highly attuned to customer needs and expectations, to be able to visualize and picture the humans for whom they are creating experiences. This goes far beyond demographics and psychographics. It's being able to picture what a given customer does and feels across their entire lifecycle with your organization. It's not just about points in time, and it's more than how they buy. It's how their needs for your product or service arise. It's about understanding what happens between when the need arises and when they finally decide to do something about it. It's about how they buy, yes. More specifically, it's about how they get acquainted with your product, how they use it for the first time, how they get more advanced with it, and how they get help using it.

Organizations need to be able to picture an actual human going through all of these experiences and be able to see what the customer sees and feel what they feel. This perspective taking is an essential component of being able to create experiences that positively impact customers, that truly help them across the lifecycle.

Empathy insights in practice means when making website decisions, sales decisions, or retail decisions, you can picture the person you are creating those experiences for. You know how they feel, what they're dealing with, what their pain points are. Even without the answer in front of you, you can make well-informed extrapolations based on what you know about that person. And—critically—other team members across the organization are picturing the same person.

In our experience, there is only one way to get to the level of depth required for empathy, and that's through one-on-one deep dive conversations with customers. Budgets universally prefer quantitative methods, as do people who believe in quantity over quality. But we ardently advocate for leading with qualitative methodologies (which can always be reinforced through quantitative research later) because it's the only real way to understand how the rational and the emotional work together. It's the only way to achieve high-fidelity perspective-taking.

When we conduct qualitative research for Strategic CX topics, the conversations are structured but leave room to wander and follow the customer's train of thought. While we always use a structured interview guide with questions and prescribed conversation flows, ultimately what we are trying to achieve is being able to picture and visualize in our minds what the customer is doing or has done related to a specific experience.

If we're interested in learning about the lead-up to an outpatient procedure, for instance, we will ask about the preceding experience ("Tell us about what led to needing outpatient care"). This information gives us context—a running start—for the experience we're seeking to dissect. Then we'll ask the patient about the very first time they were informed they needed a procedure. "How did that make you feel? What did you do? What did you do next?" We get the customer in that headspace and we lock in, exploring all details, again with the goal of being able to see what they see and feel what they feel. The more we can understand their experience, the better we can create future experiences that have impact.

Once we have gathered insights from a sample of customers, those get synthesized into a composite perspective on the customer experience in which the customer is brought to life. To accelerate stakeholder adoption and internalization, you have to get these rich insights out of a PowerPoint deck and into a framework that is more easily consumed by the organization.

The most effective framework for bringing empathy insights to life is through customer experience maps and personas. Keep in mind we build these artifacts not merely to build the artifacts or because other companies are building them or because they are deemed best practices. We build the artifacts to affect change in the company, hopefully enterprise-wide change. So while we share here how we build these artifacts, we always do so with the end intention in mind, not militantly adhering to some industry standard. We're sharing what works.

Customer Experience Maps

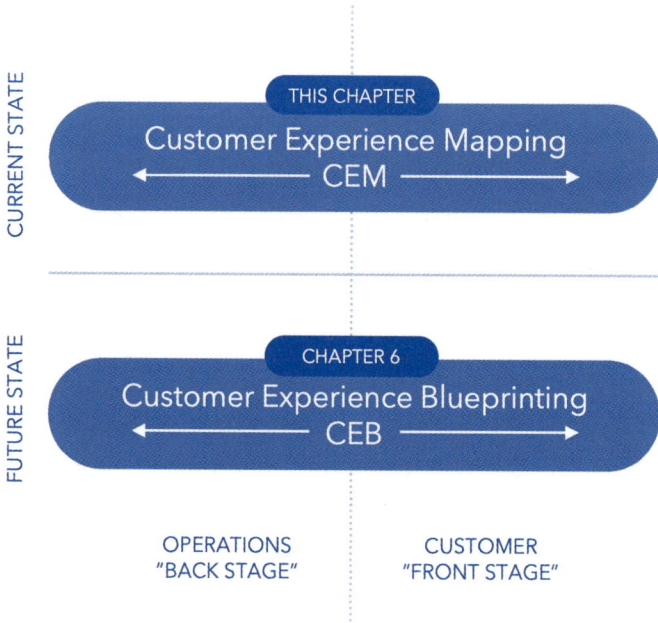

Figure 4.1: CEM and CEB

You've undoubtedly heard the term customer journey map. We use the term customer experience map (CEM) simply because it's more relatable. "Journey" connotes either some long, arduous process or an odyssey, some sort of spiritual pursuit. What you really want to understand and visualize are all of the various experiences customers have with your company and your products and also with related experiences that happen behind the curtain where you don't see them.

Ultimately we need to understand the current state of a) what the customer sees and b) what the company does and also the future state of c) what the customer will see and

d) what the company will do. We handle the current state through customer experience maps (CEMs) and future state through customer experience blueprints (CEBs). CEMs also need to represent both front stage (what the customer sees) and backstage (how the organization delivers experiences). Figure 4.1 lays this out for clarity.

Customer experience maps are easy to understand because they represent the experience a customer goes through in real life—like we all do naturally. We do one thing, then another thing, and so on sequentially over time. This timeline orientation is really helpful in seeing all aspects of what the customer sees. Doing this kind of mapping reveals really interesting opportunities for CX improvement, not just improving what the organization is doing today but also identifying new territory for customer experiences.

A simple example of experience mapping revealing opportunities for improvement is the music airlines play during the boarding process. From a CX perspective, airlines have traditionally been organized by gate operations (the experience of waiting in the gate area) and in-flight service (the flight itself). At some point in the not so distant past, someone realized a) passengers also stand in line in the jetway, and that's an opportunity to communicate with customers, and b) customers also sit and await takeoff, and that's an opportunity to reduce anxiety, to distract from the agony of waiting, and to create a soothing ambiance. These are two examples of CX improvements that arise out of the process of looking at the customer perspective versus an internal functional perspective.

Whether or not improvements like these come out of CEMs is immaterial. There is no magic to CEMs, and they are not to be developed because everyone else is creating CEMs. They are simply the most effective way we have found to make sure nothing is missed when trying to understand the full expanse of the customer experience, through the eyes of the customer.

CEMs are representations of the experience customers have related to your business at some altitude. By altitude we mean the spectrum where one end is the most zoomed-out view (all products, all customers, all experiences) and the other end is the most zoomed-in view (for instance, an online registration experience for creating an account). We can define the two ends of the spectrum of CEM altitudes to illustrate the range of potential CEMs as follows in Table 4.1:

TYPE	APPLICATION	PRIMARY USES	DESCRIPTION
Enterprise CEM	Strategic	▸ Empathy ▸ Expanding CX territory	Covers the entirety of the end-to-end customer experience. May or may not be specific to the experience with your company; can represent customers in your market generally.

TYPE	APPLICATION	PRIMARY USES	DESCRIPTION
Component CEM	Tactical	▸ Revealing experience deficiencies ▸ Blueprinting experience improvements	Covers a specific stage, time period, or set of activities. Specific to engagement with your company, perhaps a specific customer type and a specific product.

Table 4.1: CEM Altitudes

Enterprise CEMs

Enterprise CEMs are the most expansive CEMs we can make. They represent zoomed-out views of the end-to-end experience at the highest altitude. CEMs typically exist at the enterprise level, meaning everyone across the business can reference the same CEM no matter the product or functional area.

We have developed such a CEM, albeit at an industry level, but it still has all of the attributes of an enterprise CEM. It's our CEM for business customers who purchase enterprise technology called the Helix Enterprise Technology Adoption Cycle (Figure 4.2).

Helix™ Enterprise Technology Adoption Cycle

Pre-Change .... Initiative .... Non-Technology Change
.... Technology Change

FORM

01 Observe
Note opportunities for strategic and operational improvement

02 Define
Prioritize required capabilities and form initiative to pursue

IMPLEMENT

03 Purchase
Architect solution and acquire required capabilities

04 Integrate
Build and implement new capabilities and business processes

IMPROVE

05 Use
Use the capabilities to support business processes

06 Expand
Use the capabilities more deeply and more broadly

	CUSTOMER MILESTONES	VENDOR MILESTONES
01 Observe	Opportunities identified	Awareness
02 Define	Budget approval	Budget approval
03 Purchase	Capabilities procured	Purchase complete
04 Integrate	Successful Implementation	Go live
05 Use	Process improvement	Reference customer
06 Expand	Business improvement	Renewal

Figure 4.2: Helix Enterprise Technology Adoption Cycle

This is simply a high-level representation. Underpinning this are 246 activities that business customer roles perform across the experience and across a range of buyer, implementer, developer, and end-user roles. But even at this altitude, it offers myriad value. The Helix Enterprise Technology Adoption Cycle does the following:

▶ Visualizes the customer perspective: Most functional areas see their slice of the experience. By seeing the entire picture laid out end to end, teams can have a better appreciation for what the customer experiences and see potential connection points to other cross-functional team experiences.

▶ Expands the field of play: Companies can choose to (or not to) create experiences more substantially at the bookends of the experience, where the company can sow the seeds of relationship development in Observe (which, in enterprise technology, can be years before purchase) or in Expand, where adoption can take even deeper root to deliver increased value to customer organizations.

▶ Balances perspective: Most experience-mapping efforts overindex on the purchase. By including all aspects of the experience, companies can begin to appreciate that the purchase is only a piece of the puzzle.

Even for a company with thousands of products, you can create a single CEM. They are comprehensive in nature, yes, but they don't have to cover every long-tail product or fringe use case. The job of customer experience mapping is to cover a substantial enough portion of the middle of the bell curve of products in use but not necessarily both ends of the bell curve. And although people always ask, "What about product *x*?" or say, "But our market is different," stakeholders always come around in the end because they recognize when they see the CEM that things really don't differ as much as they anticipated, at least on the CEM level. (Naturally, this depends on the company. You can't build a single CEM for Philips that accommodates light bulbs and medical imaging equipment, for instance. But in health care, you can cover a doctor's visit for the common cold and knee replacement surgery in a single CEM.)

Enterprise CEMs cover the entirety of a potential customer lifecycle. While it's a timeline-based horizontal view, it's really a cycle where needs are always arising that require some sort of product. We use a horizontal visualization because it's easier to work with given the practicalities of how organizations work: on rectangular screens and rectangular slides.

As such, CEMs begin well in advance of the customer recognizing they have a problem and need a solution. It starts with the routine of life or routine of business and then flows into a need arising. CEMs extend through purchase, initial usage, and routine usage until it circles back to another purchase.

Component CEMs

Component CEMs are more focused on a specific section of the end-to-end customer experience. This can be based on a certain phase (e.g., Purchase), set of activities (e.g., customer onboarding), or activity (e.g., logging into an online account).

Although enterprise and component CEMs can both inform CX execution, it's the level of specificity that delineates these two ends of the spectrum.

Component CEMs penetrate further into the customer experience, down to the most specific details. In the earlier airline example, it would be a component CEM that would most vividly reveal the jetway and boarding experience gap and therefore inform the solutions to that unmet, unspoken customer need because, likely, an experience team would have been focused on improving the boarding experience (as opposed to addressing the total end-to-end airline experience).

CEM Characteristics

CEMs are highly effective empathy tools because of the following characteristics:

- ▶ CEMs look through the lens of the customer—their words, their actions.
- ▶ CEMs have what we call a customer "lifeflow" orientation as opposed to a product orientation. You get to look more broadly at the context of their world versus looking narrowly through the lens of the company or its products. In B2C, say, buying a car, you can map certain relevant aspects of how customers live their lives, their family situations, and their mobility needs. In B2B, say, buying a fleet of cars, you can look at how their businesses are run, the nature of their workforces, and their mobility needs.

- They are multidimensional and describe characteristics of the experience beyond just the steps in the experience. They layer in emotions, mindsets, channels, content—whatever the nature of the CEM objective demands.
- They include critical metadata about what occurs in each phase of the experience. "Think, feel, do" is a handy way to think about what to represent underneath each stage. There can be more information captured, but at a minimum, organizations need to reflect the following (Figure 4.3):

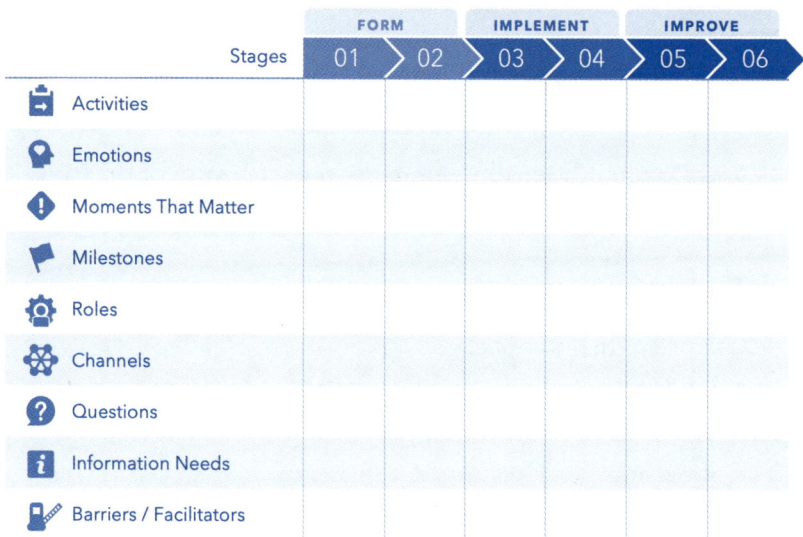

Stages	FORM		IMPLEMENT		IMPROVE	
	01	02	03	04	05	06
Activities						
Emotions						
Moments That Matter						
Milestones						
Roles						
Channels						
Questions						
Information Needs						
Barriers / Facilitators						

Figure 4.3: CEM Structure

▷ *Stages.* This is simply a way to simplify the complexity and to ease the way into making sense of the experience. In expansive CEMs, for instance, you can think of these as the big buckets of the experience. There are typically around six of them. For buying a car, these could be something like **Live** (life and mobility), **Observe** (the market for mobility), **Explore** (makes and models), **Buy** (car and ancillary services), **Use** (car and technology), and **Maintain** (routine and exceptions). For component CEMs, this could be **Online Search, Showroom Visit, Test Drive, Negotiation, Purchase, Receive Vehicle.**

▷ *Activities*. The key steps within each stage. This helps convey what occurs in each stage and gets you to the next level of specificity but, most importantly, creates the anchor for all metadata that follows (although this will exist in a separate XL database separate from the CEM visual). Within the CEM, however, activities help describe the stage. Using the car-buying example, for an expansive CEM, activities in the **Observe** stage could be along the lines of "Stay up to speed on new car makes and models," "Learn about emerging onboard technology," and "Attend car shows."

▷ *Emotions*. Potential positive and negative emotions customers exhibit along the experience. Far beyond the "smiley face/frowny face" line charts that typically represent emotions, CX Practitioners need to understand, at a minimum, the specific emotions per stage. Labeling the emotions helps bring specificity to CX execution. Hope, optimism, excitement; anxiety, frustration, embarrassment. This is the level of specificity required.

▷ *Moments that Matter.* Moments that matter can be a tricky term to pin down. It's subjective, but it refers to moments that are critical to the customer in the experience. We call them tent pole experiences because they are the ones that—if you were to look across the entirety of the customer experience—stand out as most important. In the car business, J. D. Power has quantitatively determined that warmly welcoming in customers to the dealer is critical to the dealer experience. It's a moment that matters. Without that insight, it's probably not even a thought. But armed with that information, dealers can intentionally craft a welcome experience that is impactful.

▷ *Milestones.* Milestones typically correspond to the end point of stages. They give us tangible markers for customer position and progress across the experience. Using the car example again, for an expansive CEM, the milestone at the end of the **Observe** stage could be "Decision to buy a different car." Milestones are always interesting to parse and define because you can then line up your company's milestones to see the extent to which they diverge. In this hypothetical Observe stage, for instance, the customer eventually transitions mentally from "I'm fine with my current car" to "I want to look for a new car." Mental mobilization has occurred. Has the company done what they need to do throughout that stage to help the customer along? Or has the company had the implicit milestone of forcing customers through a purchase funnel? Adopting one milestone over the other drives a lot of different choices, decisions, and actions on the part of the company.

▷ *Roles*. More often than not, there are multiple roles involved across a customer experience. This occurs more expansively in B2B, where there may be multiple senior executives, decision-makers, users, and support staff. But in B2C as well, we may have spouses, partners, friends, and others involved across the experience. Knowing who plays a role and when across the CEM helps CX Practitioners to orchestrate experiences accordingly.

▷ *Channels*. Digital is ever present across the experience, but other channels may pop in and out. Retail, salesperson interaction, support team interaction, and other engagement channels typically only appear in certain stages.

▷ *Questions*. Knowing what questions customers have in each activity helps inform blueprint development, playbook development, content development, and physical space development. It helps you know how to help customers move forward in the experience.

▷ *Information Needs.* Similarly, knowing what information customers require at each activity helps inform experience design generally and content requirements specifically, including types of information required and preferred formats (e.g., web page, PDF, video)

▷ *Barriers.* Things that can impede or slow down the customer's forward progress through the experience according to their needs and expectations, meaning they get to define what is a point of friction or not. You may think you've created a great web experience with expert tools and detailed content, but if customers say they can't find what they're looking for when they need it, then it's a barrier.

▷ *Facilitators.* Factors that help move customers along the experience: things they deem valuable and things they like about the experience. In contrast to Barriers, Facilitators are the positive aspects of the experience that facilitate progress.

CEM Benefits

CEMs offer compelling benefits:

▸ They paint a longitudinal perspective, meaning you can see the true realities of the experience through the lens of a given customer going through the end-to-end process versus what companies are set up to see, which is a silo-based slice of the experience.

- They expand the territory for customer experience efforts by considering lateral and contextual experiences to the core experience. For example, a car ownership experience may start in the years preceding the need for a new car and extend throughout routine car usage. It may contain elements of service, maintenance, care, learning, even travel. Or, zooming into onboarding for a new car experience, it may also be revealed how the primary owner educates the rest of the family on key aspects of car operation and enjoyment.
- They convey the information in a relatable model. CEMs are on a time-based continuum; everyone understands timelines.
- They provide a common language across functions. They allow for various teams to point to the same artifact and talk about the same experience elements. This inherently improves communication and collaboration.
- In their simplest forms—and this may be one of the most immediate and important impacts—CEMs bring the customer into the room and remind people they're here to create value for customers, that there are customers on the other side of the experiences they are creating. This may sound weird. It's not. As we posit, companies mistakenly tend toward misfocused management, managing processes versus intentionally delivering experiences and value. A CEM begins the path toward pivoting away from misplaced management to customer centricity.

When customer experience maps rose to prominence, they were organization-centric: focused on the company's language or the company's goals. For instance, CEMs would have stages with internal labels such as Awareness, Consideration, and Purchase. But no customer would say they are in the Awareness stage. And the CEMs zeroed in on the purchase process. The stages would parse out the purchase process and then have one single stage called Post-Purchase. As we like to say, you spend less than 1 percent of your time buying Excel and 99 percent of your time using Excel. So experience maps really need to cover the entirety of the customer experience because there are revenue and cost reduction opportunities throughout the experience, not just during the original purchase.

Experience maps also need to reflect the customers' point of view, including their language. We have always advocated for this construct. It has taken time, but companies are increasingly adopting this perspective on experience maps. It's opening a whole new world of possibilities for them.

Importantly, CEMs are based on real customer research and data. We don't make things up. Mostly they are derived from customer interviews, but CEMs can also include information and data from other sources, such as NPS or CSAT open ends, website behavioral data, and quantitative surveys.

Bringing the Customer to Life: Personas

Personas humanize the customers going through the CEMs. They bring customers to life. Remember, they exist to remind CX Practitioners every day that there are humans on the other side of the experiences they are creating. They are not meant to provide all the answers (e.g., whether a customer wants to view a piece of content via PDF or via video). Rather, they are meant to humanize and provide texture, to allow CX Practitioners to connect with customers as humans, not in the abstract as actors interacting with an asset. The data contained within a persona really depends on the persona use case. Often personas include basic demographics (e.g., age, socioeconomic status, geographic location), family situation (B2C), firmographics (B2B), what they care about, what motivates them, tech savviness, and other relevant information.

Whereas CEM metadata is fairly standard across companies, Persona metadata tends to be a bit more varied. There is a pretty significant B2C/B2B divergence, and persona insights need to be customized based on company context and how the personas will be used. Generally, personas should include the information found in Table 4.2.

B2C	B2B
▸ Photo, name, representative quote (actual quote from research)	▸ Photo, name, representative quote (actual quote from research)
▸ Family situation	▸ Job description and key responsibilities
▸ Work situation (job/career)	▸ Job priorities
▸ Involvement related to the company's product category	▸ Likes/dislikes core and adjacent to the company's product category
▸ Likes/dislikes core and adjacent to the company's product category	▸ Career aspirations
▸ Life aspiration	▸ Role across the lifecycle
▸ Role across the lifecycle	

Table 4.2: Persona Metadata

Personas can be more detailed, depending on altitude and use. For instance, a persona tied to an enterprise CEM might have the data listed in Table 4.2, whereas a persona tied to a component CEM might include more detailed information about product feature usage, product use cases, and channel interactions. Personas can capture whatever makes the most sense for how they are going to be used. The most important thing to keep in mind is you're simply creating a centralized vehicle for shared customer understanding within and across functional areas. Personas capture a customer's humanity, replacing the need for each CX Practitioner to piece together their own composite view of the customer from traditional data sources.

Like CEMs, personas are based on real customer research and data. Again, they are mostly derived from customer interviews but can also include information and data from other sources as well.

Personas vs. Segmentation

We are often asked the difference between customer personas and customer segmentation. Customer segmentation is the practice of dividing either your customer base and/or the addressable market into groups similar across some set of attributes to a) make the market a bit easier to identify with and b) enable tailored outreach.

There are many types of segmentations, including:

- Demographic segmentation (divides customers based on demographic factors such as age, gender, income, education, occupation, marital status, and family size)
- Psychographic segmentation (focuses on customers' psychological characteristics, lifestyle, values, beliefs, interests, hobbies, personality traits, and attitudes)
- Behavioral segmentation (segments customers based on their behavior, usage patterns, buying habits, and interactions with the brand)
- Firmographic segmentation (used in B2B contexts, segments customers based on firmographic factors such as industry, company size, revenue, location, and organizational structure)

Segmentation efforts and usage live primarily in marketing departments, and they have primarily been used in the same way since the advent of segmentation: to drive purchase funnel marketing activities. Building a segmentation model is a highly quantitative exercise. It's not built for empathy but for operations.

In an ideal B2C world, there would be a one-to-one mapping of persona to segment, with the persona bringing humanity and empathy into the equation. (In B2B, this is made more complicated by the fact that segmentation is usually done on factors that don't allow for one-to-one mapping.) But there's a lot of confusion on how personas and segmentations work together or not. There's really no standard here and a lot of "it depends":

- It depends on the type of segmentation. If the segmentation is demographic, for instance, that will be hard to match up with a set of personas, which are ideally based on experiential needs and behaviors.

- It depends on why the segmentation was created. If the segmentation was spearheaded by marketing for media planning or targeting purposes, then it may not line up with personas because personas should be created with the end-to-end experience in mind.

- It depends on how broadly the segmentation is known and understood across the organization. If the segmentation is deployed only by marketing but other areas of the business refer to the segments as an empathy tool, then personas may have to align to the segments versus if the segmentation is only used by and known to marketing.

Generally speaking, it's okay if the segmentation and personas don't map one to one. Segmentation is used for one set of purposes, typically not for CX work, while personas are used to humanize customers for experience development purposes.

CEMs and Personas Replace Guesswork

Understanding customers across the entire lifecycle via CEMs and personas is not only a key requirement of CX excellence, but it also makes it easier for CX Practitioners to do their work. Without empathy insights, you're left with guessing, making things up, and working off an individualized perspective of the customer. Erroneous assumptions are made; everyone has a belief that their understanding of the customer is the right understanding of the customer. There's fruitless debate on what the customer wants and needs. With empathy insights in the form of CEMs and personas, however, there is the same shared view of the customer across teams, and that view is based on research.

An issue that companies run into, however, is that no one single CEM and no single set of personas can cover all macro and micro experiences and customer segments. They can't cover every use case, every product, every region, every industry, every channel. This is true, and that's okay. What an end-to-end CEM and a set of top-level personas can do, however, is establish an orienting framework against which team-specific CEMs and personas can be created. It's simply unreasonable and unrealistic for an entire organization to adopt only one CEM and only one set of personas. Those will be rejected by the organizational system. CX Practitioners won't believe in them, they won't be invested in them, and they won't trust them. But they are likely to accept top-line artifacts at face value and then snap their specific efforts to them.

For instance—and we have done this—you can build a component CEM for the login experience to software and how users manage multiple account logins and passwords. That experience can be connected conceptually to the larger enterprise CEM as a way of understanding what's going on laterally in the experience for that user: What has led up to this moment, and what comes after this moment? In this case, the specific team designing the login experience gains the value of building their own view in an area they oversee, and the organization gains the value of cross-team coordination and alignment associated with all component CEMs laddering up to the enterprise CEM.

Used together, CEMs and personas constitute a powerful canvas of CX opportunity. They reveal the porous nature of the current state experiences the company's delivering and illuminate the opportunities to deliver greater value to customers.

Connecting Front Stage to Backstage

Up to this point, we have discussed the importance of customer insights and the artifacts that bring them to life. Another set of components that are incredibly helpful and powerful to add are the current state backstage counterparts to the current state front stage customer experience.

When we talk about backstage, what we mean is all of the internal machinery that results in what a customer sees, feels, touches, and experiences. It includes all of the resources, assets, and skills the organization marshals to deliver customer experiences, namely:

▶ *Functional coverage.* Which functional areas play a role in delivering various experiences.
▶ *Processes.* The processes the company executes to deliver and enable customer experiences. In health care, this could be the process to gather new patient information. In banking, this could be the process for cross-selling mortgage products to existing customers.

- *Initiatives*. Planned, funded, or in-progress initiatives that will modify or change existing processes.
- *Metrics*. How the company tracks success or progress across the experience.
- *Content*. The content the company currently provides against each activity in the CEM.
- *Technology*. Key technologies that are leveraged to enable experiences.
- *Data*. Sources and types of data leveraged to enable experiences.

Because CEMs are designed to bring empathy with the customer as well as enlightenment of what the customer reality is, we also can take this opportunity to map internal dimensions within the context of the CEM. To complete a well-rounded view of the current state, we map backstage components to the customer experience as additional swim lanes. This helps build a connection from what will at first be a seemingly distant, somewhat unfamiliar external world (although that perspective will change by virtue of this new empathy tool) to what is known and familiar—internal operations.

When you line up each of the aforementioned areas in the context of the customer experience, it reveals areas of overlap (e.g., too many functions addressing the same set of customer activities), gaps (e.g., no content to support a set of customer activities), or insufficiencies (e.g., not enough support for a given set of customer activities).

The process of mapping the backstage experience is as much a benefit to the organization as is the actual map artifact. The process brings together people who normally don't interact, brings cross-functional awareness to what everyone does and is working on, and builds a comprehensive view of the CX-related inner workings of the organization (or, in the case of component CEMs, of a slice of the organization).

Building an awareness and understanding of the operational practices, processes, programs, and people entails internal deep dive meetings, document reviews, and analyses to uncover all of this information. Mapping backstage for enterprise CEMs is less intense than mapping backstage for component CEMs. In enterprise CEMs, you are seeking a wide-ranging, high-level perspective on the broad strokes. In component CEMs, you may have to do, say, a content audit to really understand what is available for customers, but not always. Or you may need to do a heuristic review of a web experience to understand what you're working with on a page by page, user flow basis. So the level of depth varies by the nature of how the organization is going to be using the CEM in question.

Once the backstage is laid bare in the context of the customer experience, you can see where you may have too much or too little coverage of certain aspects of the end-to-end experience. You can also see where you may have the right process or program in place but at the wrong point of the experience.

For instance, we worked with a client in the wholesale consumer goods space who had been delivering their onboarding program later than it should have been—after the first purchase from a new customer instead of before the first purchase, where it would have more value and impact as part of internal change management efforts. Some individual sales and account representatives probably knew about this shortcoming, but until enough of the right decision-makers hear this from enough customers, those types of changes are less likely to get enacted. They will certainly not happen as quickly as if they had been revealed during a serious effort to improve the customer experience.

Having both a front stage and backstage view allows CX Practitioners to see the whole board and understand the extent to which the entire system is in alignment. From this perspective, you can understand the current state with great fidelity and then determine what you want the future state to look like (see chapter 6 on customer experience blueprinting).

Insights Adoption

With CEM and personas completed, those insights need to be onboarded into the organization. One of the most critical factors for insights adoption is priming the organization by including CX Champions or key CX Practitioners in the research process from the very beginning. Ideally they would be included in the research objective setting, learning agenda, research observation, and readouts. Many people tend not to fully participate, but simply being given that option and having some sense of control or influence in the process reduces resistance once the research findings, CEM, and personas are delivered. They feel like a participant, not a recipient.

No one can simply read a CEM and persona and get the customer. CX Practitioners need to install these insights into the organization as immersively as possible. There are a number of ways this can be executed in a way that is specific to company culture. From workshops to videos to online tools to posters, CX Practitioners need to make the insights highly consumable and easy to internalize.

Once the insights are installed in the organization, they then need to be used in practice. They need to be the default tool without which teams refuse to go forward. Insights need to be sought after, leveraged, and applied in the work—in meetings, in ideation, in design, and in process execution. They are constant companions, referred to innately, implicitly, and explicitly. How does that work in practice? Our clients who have adopted personas, for instance, refer to them by their proper first names in meetings:

▶ "Well, Ryan needs this from us at this point because he's anxious about whether or not the product will truly function, so we need to provide x."
▶ "We're targeting Ashley at this point because she is leading the decision process."
▶ "We need to make sure we have something for Donna because she is the one who actually goes to the website to look for information."

We also need to build habits. Some things we have found to be successful include:

▶ Visuals around the office, visuals in PowerPoint decks, visuals in town hall meetings, and in myriad other settings creates repetition and triggers connection to people's everyday work.

- ▶ Continuous reinforcement of why insights matter, how they are used, and the impact they drive all help people understand the *why* behind the artifacts.
- ▶ Digital accessibility via a company intranet provides another means of access to the insights.
- ▶ Leadership advocacy and encouragement to frame activities and plans in the context of the customer experience provides yet another dimension of motivation to adopt insights.

Empathy insights, CEMs, and personas in and of themselves are not enough. Following through to ensure organizational adoption is critical to enable teams to operate with the best insights possible to drive CX efforts.

Insights Maintenance

The world is changing fast, so insights need to be enriched, updated, and refreshed on a routine basis. There are no hard and fast rules around maintenance cadence. It generally depends on a) budget, b) appetite, and c) CEM and persona altitude. Component CEMs are easier to update than enterprise CEMs simply because of the territory covered. Enterprise CEMs cover so much territory for so many customer types that updating them is more time-consuming and costly than doing so for component CEMs. Also, enterprise CEMs are used by more people than component CEMs, so we don't want to update those too frequently. Otherwise, the organization has to relearn those enterprise CEMs.

We encourage companies to start the process of refreshing

the enterprise CEMs the moment they feel they are beginning to feel outdated. We do this because:

1. We don't know in advance when they are going to start to feel outdated, and if we refresh too soon, it might not be worth the investment.
2. Often companies start to feel enterprise CEMs are outdated way before they actually are, giving companies the lead time to plan, fund, and conduct the research required to update them.
3. It helps justify asking the organization to replace the enterprise CEM with a new one.

Refresh cadence for component CEMs varies by the time horizon of the CX initiatives tied to the component CEMs. Some initiatives are tied to executions that are very defined and take under a year to implement (say, simplifying the online checkout process), in which case the component CEM may not need to be updated at all. Other initiatives will take longer to solve (say, new customer onboarding), in which case pieces of them may need to be updated.

It's critical to have CEMs in the first place to get the organization used to building empathy with customers. Updating them is a separate dimension of importance to make sure that the insights are current and relevant.

The organization will go through a typical maturity curve as more and more CX Practitioners learn how insights are applied in everyday decision-making. CX Practitioners will be more comfortable and fluent with the insights. It takes time, but with continuous advocacy by CX Champions, we have seen CEMs and personas truly take hold in global companies of massive scale. And when they do, organizations begin to use them in many unforeseen ways, which is what we want to see—that hunger for and belief in high-value customer insights. Next, let's talk about the strategy surrounding CX that will get everyone moving in the same direction.

BEFORE & AFTER

Before Insights: Insight Gaps

An education technology client was operating with traditional customer insights: NPS, CSAT, product research, etc. These insights were research-study centric, not customer centric. They lived in reports, isolated from one another and confined to the teams that commissioned the research. Each customer-facing functional area was serving customers according to their best abilities with their own view of the customer they felt was accurate, extrapolating and filling in blind spots with their own assumptions. This was not done with ill intentions, but without anything else to go on, each function and each person within each function had their own perspective on the customer they were serving. CX Practitioners had to design experiences without critical insights about customer needs, expectations, behaviors, and emotions. At best, they were creating experiences that met an assumption about rational needs and only for their sliver of the experience. At worst, they were creating experiences that repelled customers.

After Insights: Full-Bodied Perspective

Armed with empathy insights across the experience, our client was able to see the whole humans they were serving with products, information, training, and assistance. Through experience maps, they were able to see where handoffs were failing, where customer needs existed that weren't being served, and where they could provide additional value to help customers achieve their objectives. Processes were added, moved, and/or improved accordingly. Empathy was injected into customer experiences, addressing emotional needs like fear, anxiety, anticipation, and joy. The customer experience became more than a series of disconnected interactions.

Key Points Recap

▶ CX Practitioners need to be able to picture in their mind's eye the humans for whom they are creating experiences.

▶ CEMs and personas are great ways to not only represent empathy insights in a highly usable and understandable format, but they also create a central source of truth for various teams to reference.

▶ Market and competitive conditions change; companies launch new products and acquire new companies. Insights need to be kept current and refreshed with regularity.

With the types and role of insights defined, we can turn next to CX strategy and see how it can serve to coordinate and align cross-functional CX efforts.

CHAPTER 5 OVERVIEW

TOPIC PREVIEW	▸ CX strategy establishes a vision, points everyone in the same direction, and guides cross-functional teams forward together.
	▸ A CX strategy is essential for coordinating and aligning CX efforts across the enterprise or within a functional area.
	▸ CX strategy is about choice and focus; it's about what you will and won't do.
What we mean by **STRATEGY**	CX strategy (CXS) defines how the organization will leverage its collective capabilities and navigate complexity to compete and win on customer experience. The CXS articulates the future organization wants and how to get there. It is rooted in a deep analysis of a range of factors and is therefore carefully developed to be unique to the organization.
Why **STRATEGY** *is important*	With a CXS in place, teams are able to execute with a shared direction and principles, resulting in a more integrated experience for customers. Without it, teams execute according to their own beliefs and inclinations, resulting in a disjointed, uneven customer experience.
With **STRATEGY...**	The organization can execute in lockstep in a defined direction, with guardrails on how to execute.
Without **STRATEGY...**	Teams execute point experiences without laddering up to a common higher order purpose.

5

STRATEGIC PRACTICE TWO: STRATEGY

Creating a Winning North Star

As mentioned previously in the chapter "The Case for CX," the work of CX is already happening across the company every day by myriad teams who, as in the CPG example, may not only be disconnected but are also often unaware of each other's work. The various teams that comprise the sum total of CX work are not completely aware of the full extent of lateral experiences that are created every day. Even within a single function—say, marketing—the vast majority of people would not be aware of all of the CX-related programs that its own function produces (in the case of marketing, campaigns, events, newsletters, CRM, etc.).

Consequently, CX delivery is happening in silos and, to varying degrees, leading to disparities across the customer experience. Organizations may be overindexing in certain stages, under-indexing in other stages, and absent in other parts of the experience. Most organizations are not load balancing across the customer lifecycle, and all too often they are putting customers on an expectations trajectory in the prepurchase stages that cannot be met in the post-purchase stages. Customers also have to navigate their way through the experience, traverse experience obstacles, and fend for themselves during unsupported gaps.

Essentially, there is little coordination across CX delivery teams. Each team is delivering according to their own ideas about what experiences to create for customers. We find that this work is by and large well intentioned. It's just not coordinated in such a way that a customer slicing through those experiences would say they have a valuable, smooth, and consistent end-to-end experience.

A CX strategy addresses these shortcomings. A CXS thoroughly and critically analyzes external and internal conditions, identifies obstacles and points of leverage, establishes a direction for CX, and serves as a coordination, alignment, and connectivity layer across CX teams. The strategy represents an integrated set of choices that provides teams with forward direction together and is purpose-built for what will best serve the customer and the company.

A CXS does this by articulating a focal point for the customer experience the organization wants to create. Strategy sets the direction, creates clarity, coordinates action, and navigates obstacles. It defines how the organization will deliver value in accordance with internal guardrails. A CXS serves a vital role in bringing focus and clarity to a wide set of efforts performed by a variety of individuals across the organization. With a CXS in place, teams are all pointed in the same direction. Without it, even if great experiences are being created, there is little chance that everyone will be unified along a common path.

The CXS also creates a center of gravity to guide all teams on CX initiatives and execution. It is a way for leadership to know innately what the body of work is about, to help coordinate resources, to help prioritize investment: to stitch together an integrated CX that covers the chosen playing field. This allows them to always have the direction in their head—a way to pursue initiatives that make sense and say no to those that don't.

In our experience, a customer experience strategy is essential for aligning teams, coordinating efforts, and maintaining a chosen trajectory for CX. A CXS strives to bring silos and sub-silos together so that everyone is moving in the same direction. We believe that strategy is meaningful, powerful, and clarifying. It's essential to moving teams and organizations forward together from point A to point B. In the right hands that have an understanding of how to use it, a CXS can be one of the most powerful means for accomplishing CX excellence. A well-crafted CX strategy sets the path forward and unifies teams with a common objective.

Companies can struggle with CX strategy because:

▸ They don't understand its purpose and how it's used.
▸ They don't make tough choices; rather, they try to accommodate all stakeholder needs at once.
▸ They skip it entirely and go straight to tactics.

We believe it's a critical mistake to bypass or avoid the hard work of strategy development. To us, it's essential as a springboard to a well-oiled CX machine

WHAT IS STRATEGY?

Strategy is a misunderstood term, so much so that it is a dirty word in some organizations. People often skip right past this step. They generally do not want to invest the time in strategy development because they've seen the lack of results of such efforts, thus perpetuating the myth that working on strategy is a waste of time. It's a waste of time when done poorly. When done correctly, it is instrumental in coordinating, guiding, aligning, and directing CX work across efforts.

Let's take a moment to broadly define what strategy is. One of the best books on the topic of strategy is called *Good Strategy, Bad Strategy,* by Richard Rumelt. It identifies the hallmarks of great strategy. For instance:

- Good strategy emanates from a smart diagnosis of the situation, from identifying one or two critical issues in the situation. It honestly acknowledges the challenges being faced and provides an approach to overcoming them. The diagnosis should simplify the complexity of the situation. Different diagnoses of the exact same situation can lead to radically different paths, so this is a critical analysis.

- Good strategy conveys how the organization will navigate complexity and challenges. It "directs and constrains action without fully defining its content."
- Good strategy is simple and obvious and does not require a set of PowerPoint slides to explain.
- Good strategy leans into the pivot points that can multiply the effectiveness of effort—and then focuses and concentrates action and resources on them. It applies leverage to where it will have the greatest effect.

What people often deem strategy either isn't strategy at all. Strategy is not stating what the organization is going to do—that's the job of the strategic plan. Strategy is not stating what the organization's ambitions are—that's the job of objectives and goals. Simply stated, strategy is about identifying the critical factors and obstacles in a situation and designing a way of coordinating and focusing actions to deal with those factors and obstacles.

What people also often call strategy comes out of a process that doesn't lead to strategy. When strategy goes wrong, it is most often because a) strategy is reverse engineered to put packaging around what the organization is already doing, and/or b) the strategy is too broad, accommodating everyone's wishes so that no one's feathers are ruffled.

Often organizations do not want to take the time to develop a strategy because strategy overwhelmingly is about what they are not going to do much more than it is about what they are going to do. Choice and focus are at the heart of strategy. The strategy can't be the average of what everyone in the organization wants. That's how you get to strategy that isn't strategy. Strategy is built through a process of assessing the situation, coming to a clear diagnosis, and then determining how to leverage our strengths to navigate complexity. As *Good Strategy, Bad Strategy* notes, "There is difficult psychological, political, and organizational work in saying 'no' to whole worlds of hopes, dreams, and aspirations."

Relationship with Other Enterprise-Level Strategies

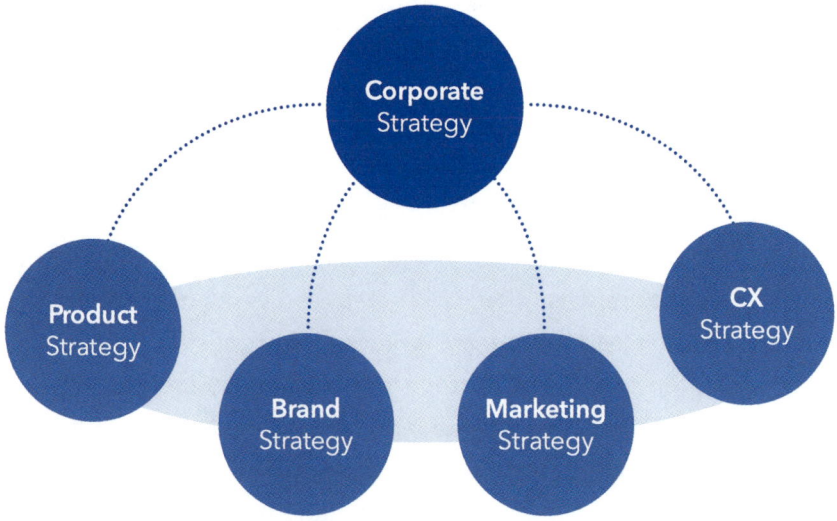

Figure 5.1: CX Analysis Map

CX strategy has a very specific role relative to some of the other organizational strategies typically in place, namely corporate strategy, product strategy, brand strategy, and marketing strategy (Figure 5.1). These types of strategies are mature practices and are known entities. And the goal of CX Champions is to advance the customer agenda in the organization with as little friction as possible. Therefore, the CXS needs to be purely additive, harmonize with these other strategies, and not cause friction or infighting. It's an exercise of threading the needle.

Furthermore, the CXS does not have to take on too much of the burden relative to other enterprise-level strategies because these strategies have already wrestled with some very tough topics in their own right and provide excellent inputs for CX strategy:

- The corporate strategy already defines the business the company is in, how it'll generate profits, where it'll prioritize its collective efforts, who it'll target, and what geographic markets it'll focus on.
- The product strategy prioritizes areas of focus and further product development.
- The brand strategy defines the value proposition and positioning—how it wants to be perceived.
- The marketing strategy defines who it'll find, reach, and engage potential and current customers.

What is not covered by these enterprise strategies (related to the customer) are:

- How the direction set by these enterprise strategies will play out and come to life for the customer

- How the company will deliver value to the customer in totality across the entirety of its relationship with them
- How it'll advance from current state CX to optimal future state CX

Therefore, the CXS needs to define:

- How the experience will feel for stakeholders
- How the company will win with stakeholders in totality
- How the company will win against the competition to deliver differentiated value
- How the company will orchestrate efforts across the business to deliver on enterprise strategies
- How the company will win at doing the work of experience internally

Organizations need to create a CXS to define the *what* and *how* of customer value delivery with intention, specificity, and precision: *what* the experiences will be and *how* they'll deliver them as an organization.

The CXS represents a set of decisions and choices that make the experience work within the context of the organization. While it is a separate artifact for management purposes, it works best not as a separate strategy at the same level as the other enterprise strategies but rather as a weaving of the customer to its rightful status as a leading business driver, coordinating and bringing to life that which is set forth in the other enterprise strategies and filling in any gaps. The CXS elevates the customer into the corporate DNA.

In our worldview, the CX strategy is derived with

guidance from the corporate strategy and brand strategy and is an input into product and marketing strategies. This is the ideal state. We recognize that CX strategy is a new discipline and most likely doesn't inform product and marketing strategies; the CX strategies we see are isolated from product and marketing strategies. But conceptually, because we view CX strategically as the entirety of what customers see, do, think, and feel about the value the company provides, we think that should set the stage for other related customer-facing functional areas.

Despite the time and attention we have just devoted in this chapter to defining strategy, we also believe organizations don't need to be militant about the definition of strategy versus objectives or plans. We ultimately want meaningful forward progress toward a better CX and therefore better business results for companies. Slowing that down to meet the gray area definitions of strategy is not in anyone's best interests. Instead, we are militant about two things:

1. Does the strategy a) establish a vision and b) serve to coordinate action across teams (does it have the characteristics of strategy)?
2. Does the strategy chart a path to a winning customer experience (is the strategy a good set of choices)?

Also, the process of strategy development itself has value. It involves people across the organization, it builds internal relationships and connections, it invests people in the work, and it's inspiring to have people think about the future we want to create.

The CX Strategic Framework

For some CX Champions and believers, it's enough to intuitively know that delivering a great experience will generate positive business results, much like some people believe in product quality without needing to prove that it's good business. But that's generally not enough for organizations to embrace new territory or do things differently. We need to set up an objectives framework to establish the *why* for the business as a financial concern, consisting of a) revenue factors, b) cost factors, and c) nonfinancial factors in a relational framework (incorporating impacts on customers, employees, and the company, as laid out in chapter 2, "The Case for CX").

Once the financial impacts have been identified, the CX strategy can be developed. There is no single agreed-upon way to devise or represent strategy. There is no magical, slick-templated answer for what a CX strategy should look like and nothing that dictates what it contains. Much of it depends on the flow of the situation and the teams involved. No matter how it is represented, though, it must do certain things to be considered a true CX strategy. After having done it numerous times with numerous clients, we have arrived at an approach that is both useful for clients and used by clients. It's not based on theory or management models. It's based on needs we see and what actually moves companies forward.

While we use the term "strategy" as a handle, there are actually several components that add up to what we call strategy. The strategy emerges and reveals itself via the totality of the CX Strategic Framework (Figure 5.2).

The CX Strategic Framework establishes where the organization is going in its CX pursuits. It plants a flag for goal attainment. It sets the aspiration and priorities for what the organization will be creating together. It's aspirational yet realistic and achievable.

We think of the CX Strategic Framework as a more static object (static but routinely revisited and refreshed; it always needs to feel current and relevant). It covers a time horizon that can be measured in years—a year at the minimum, which is based on how long it takes to affect meaningful CX progress.

Key components of the CX Strategic Framework are as follows:

1. Key Factors

It begins with an analysis of the Four C's: what customers want, what companies want, where competitors are going, and the context for where the market at large is going. There will, of course, be lots of analysis and nuance behind each of these factors, but strategy is largely subjective analysis, so it's helpful to be simple and clear at this level. (We provide detail on this analysis in this chapter under "Process for Developing CX Strategy.")

▶ Customers: Which audiences is the company focusing on, what are their characteristics, and what are their needs and expectations? Not surprisingly, this is the information created in insights work but distilled down to as simple as you're comfortable with. So simple you can write it in a sentence or two, just a quick at-a-glance characterization.

KEY FACTORS

Customers
What they care about
- struggle with (–)
- appreciate us for (+)
- feel (heart)
- expect (head)

Company
Where we're going
- strengths (+)
- weaknesses (–)
- headwinds (–)
- tailwinds (+)

Competitors
Where they're going
- strengths
- vulnerabilities

Context
Where the market and culture are going
- conditions
- trends

CX VISION

Aspirational yet achievable desired future state
+
Customer outcomes (emotional and/or rational)

HALLMARK EXPERIENCES

Key experiences that illustrate the CX Vision

Key Enablers	Priorities
Capabilities needed to deliver the CX Vision	*Centers of focus and leverage*

Experience Principles	Key Metrics
Characteristics of CX efforts	*Business impacts*

Figure 5.2: Key Components of the CX Strategic Framework

- Company: The corporate strategy, focus areas, and key objectives. Again, distilled into a few sentences.
- Competitors: Characterization of the competitive environment.
- Context: Industry dynamics, macro trends, societal changes, and regulation. No need to pore over mountains of macroeconomic data. The corporate strategy catches most of the highly complex business strategy factors. What you're seeking here is that which is relevant to the intersection of your business and customer experience.

2. Vision

We like to take a very customer outcomes–based view of the CX Vision. We like to use it to paint a picture of what customers will be experiencing and/or feeling at some achievable point in the future after the company has reached some better threshold of CX. The vision is about the customer, and even with this statement alone—without the rest of the strategic framework—a different set of decisions will be made about customer experience execution than if the vision statement was something different or more internally focused. Generally there is nowhere the company articulates how it envisions the ideal customer outcome, so start with the vision as an opportunity to establish a shared aspiration of the customer future state across the enterprise, including product and all surrounding experiences.

3. Hallmarks

Having established a sense of the desired future state, the strategy needs to bring that to life at a more relatable level to allow people to picture what this new experience may look and feel like. We like to select a handful of tent pole experiences across the customer experience that a) represent critical experiences for the customer and b) are most in need of attention, those that will likely change significantly from the current state.

4. Enablers

Moving from current state to future state will require new capabilities, new skills, and new ways of doing business—breaking out of the status quo. You need to prepare the organization for some big changes by identifying some of the most significant operational changes that will be required in terms of technology, data, processes, cross functional collaboration, driving advocacy, etc.

5. Priorities

The organization needs to determine how best to start closing the gap from current state CX to future state while leveraging and navigating the dynamics identified in Key Factors. You don't need to (and can't) prescribe all activities to get you there, but you need to really think critically about where to focus initial efforts. There will be a lot riding on these initial efforts. It's a chance to show progress to leadership and build trust in the cross-functional team. Sometimes this may mean choosing to start with the areas of greatest business impact. Sometimes this may mean choosing some of the easiest wins. Other times, it may mean choosing something to get an important advocate on board. In any case, the organization must choose its initial paths forward. You're looking for leverage points.

6. Principles

These frame key attributes that the organization will strive for in every interaction. Rooted in the unique attributes and position of the company's brand, the experience principles help create consistency and differentiation. They are attributes that can be tangibly designed and experienced in all interactions and touchpoints that a customer has with the organization, from an advertising campaign to a retail environment to a call center experience to a product. The principles help to unify and create meaningful customer connections across diverse experience modalities.

7. Key Metrics

Metrics are important in any organization, so you need to acknowledge those in the strategic framework. You can also think of this section as a change management mechanism. Metrics are a way to continue to expand how people think about CX and reinforce how CX metrics are business metrics. We like to cover three dimensions:

- *Revenue Gains.* Through more effective acquisition, retention, cross-sell, and upsell.
- *Cost Reduction.* Through consolidating duplicative efforts and eliminating ineffective efforts.
- *Nonfinancial.* Intangibles related to both customer and employee measures (e.g., experience scores, satisfaction).

Where Strategy Can Be Applied

Like CEMs described in the Insights chapter, strategy can be applied at any altitude: to the entire enterprise, to a customer segment, to part of the experience, to a channel. We advocate for enterprise-wide CX strategy to ensure a consistent, connected experience across the end-to-end customer experience. But we recognize that's not always possible as a company embarks upon its own CX journey and that it's better sometimes to start in a specific area of the business.

When we work with chief customer experience officers (CCXOs), we develop strategy at the enterprise level, which applies to all front stage and backstage functional areas. This enterprise CX strategy is akin to enterprise CEMs. When we work on CX in a specific area of the business, for instance, a marketing lead in charge of the post-purchase experience, we develop strategy for that altitude as well (akin to component CEMs).

Counterintuitively, both enterprise and component strategies feel quite similar. This is because whether you're talking about the entirety of the customer experience or a specific customer experience, you aspire to be your best and reach your highest potential. When you think about it, it's actually intuitive that both altitudes would feel similar because the aspirations and characteristics of the vertical experience have to ladder up to the horizontal experience, so by definition, they inherently overlap.

For instance, if the enterprise-wide horizontal strategy states that the company seeks to "create experiences that make the customer feel confident in their usage of the product," you can see how that would also apply to a vertical strategy in post-purchase stages. If you were creating a CX strategy for prepurchase, perhaps the CX strategy would be something around confidence that "customers are purchasing the right product for their specific needs." Still similar.

In all cases of CX execution, some sort of higher strategic purpose needs to be in place to give shape and meaning to CX efforts.

Process for Developing CX Strategy

People are generally intimidated by the prospect of developing a CX strategy, but putting a process in place provides confidence for both process owners and participants. A defined process makes the effort more tangible, becomes a unifying guidepost for the various stakeholders involved, and conveys a sense of purpose and rigor. Our process follows four key stages:

Assess

As mentioned in the Assessment chapter, embarking upon CX improvement at any level—whether focusing on a specific area of the business or an organization-wide transformation—must begin with an honest assessment of where the organization is today. Every organization does customer experience. The question is at what level? What's working, what's not working? What are the headwinds, what are the tailwinds? And crucially, how does everyone feel about all of these questions?

We start this way to make sure everyone's on the same page, to give time to reflect on the bigger narrative, the bigger picture. How do you do that? Part of it is acknowledging where you've been. The organization didn't end up where it is just by chance. A set of decisions, practices, and priorities got it to the current state. Explore and dissect that. Honor it and learn from it.

A reflection is a great way to get everyone involved, think critically about past work, and do a little organizational therapy so the organization can all move forward together without dwelling on the past. This is done by jettisoning any ill will, any grudges, and any bad taste from prior experiences and CX efforts.

This step of the process should be inclusive, bringing the people who will be leading strategy and execution and the people doing the work in from the very start.

Time permitting, this is not a one-off meeting, but rather it's at least a half-day session where the teams can talk about the state of CX relevant to the area for which the strategy is being created (remember, a strategy can be developed at any altitude).

Analyze

Our process for CX strategy development focuses on four key areas of analysis, the Four C's:

1. Customers

- ► Their needs and expectations in terms of a) the company's products, b) what gives rise to them needing the company's products, and c) the problems they are trying to solve. This broad perspective opens up new potential opportunities for the organization to consider
- ► Current experience likes and dislikes (where the organization is doing things right and where it needs improvement)
- ► Their emotions across the experience and the extent to which the organization is meeting those needs

The CEM and personas generally provide what you are looking for, plus you can leverage other insights sources that are already up and running, like NPS. When leveraging insights from various sources, it is helpful to synthesize those insights into an integrated document for reference throughout the CX strategy development process.

2. Company

- ► Vision and strategy—where the organization is going and how it'll get there. Increasingly there are clues to, if not outright mention of, the company's perspective on the customer and the customer relationship in corporate strategies. Some mention the customer as a "check the box" exercise, but more often than not, the corporate strategy gives dimension to the official corporate perspective on how it wants to win with customers, albeit with a heavy emphasis on either customer markets to pursue, products to pursue, or both (i.e., corporate strategies don't generally plot a course for connecting with and building lasting relationships with customers). You don't necessarily have to rely on the corporate strategy to significantly inform the CX strategy; rather, you need to harvest the corporate strategy for whatever guidance you can glean from it.

- Strengths and weaknesses as they relate to what impacts the customer experience and what the company is facing as an entity. This can be both front stage (e.g., product unique value proposition, service excellence, increasing competition) and backstage (e.g., established cross-functional collaboration practices, modern tech stack, staff shortages).

The corporate strategy and other key strategic documents are generally the source for this analysis.

3. Competitors

- Identification of companies that are significantly impacting customer expectations, both internal and external to your industry. At some point many years ago, we started noticing in our B2B research that customers were increasingly asking, "Why can't this experience be like Apple or Starbucks?" All of the sudden, companies not only have to live up to best in class in its industry, but they have to live up to best in class, period. Looking across industry borders to see what CX leader companies are doing helps CX Practitioners understand the bar of excellence from another angle (in addition to the customer perspective). They are all setting customer expectations that the organization needs to be aware of.

► For these competitors, you want to understand CX-related activities, improvements, and shortcomings. What experiences do they own and do uniquely well? Where are they vulnerable?

4. Context

► Broad market and cultural trends that directly or indirectly impact customer expectations, attitudes, and behaviors. For instance, the rise of home entertainment subscription services such as Hulu or Netflix has changed consumer expectations for how they access TV and movies. It was once a luxury to have a subscription service. Now it's almost mandatory.

► General movements that impact customer expectations, attitudes, and behaviors. For instance, sustainability is a global movement that has become part of nearly all companies' operations, influencing products, services, manufacturing, technology, facilities, sourcing, etc. Customers generally value sustainability efforts, which is attributable to a global movement.

These four areas, synthesized together, form the mental environmental framework for the conditions through which the vision will be established and the strategy will be set. It requires some tea leaf reading, but if the analysis and synthesis are done properly, a set of viable potential options should be waiting to be revealed.

To facilitate this analysis and enable more effective tea leaf reading, we have a CX Analysis Map (Figure 5.3), which can drive both strategy development and blueprint development.

Explore

With the analysis completed, we can begin to explore a range of options for the strategy. Depending on company culture, ambitions, and risk tolerance, the strategy can be bold (it can declare an ambitious yet achievable path), or it can be a bit more safe, which still has merit because there is nothing wrong with tightening and improving the existing CX territory.

To get a sense of what this exploration may generate, let's use an example most of us are familiar with: Starbucks. Let's say Starbucks decided to develop an enterprise-wide CX strategy (which they may or may not have—we don't know). Imagine sitting in a conference room with the following in hand:

- Customer data, which might include items such as:

  - The target market, which is relatively affluent—middle and upper class—as well as educated, socially aware, active, and busy.
  - Being of high socioeconomic status and professionally driven, Starbucks's target audience are busy achievers

and explorers with budget to spare and spend. They place value in the brands they choose, are health conscious, are socially aware, and care about the environment.

▷ Chief complaints center around long wait times, inconsistent quality, and store cleanliness.

▸ A corporate strategy document, which might include items such as:

▷ Investing in purpose-built store concepts, including diversifying and expanding store formats.

▷ Delivering beverage innovation, including equipment innovation designed to meet the growing demand for customization.

▷ Expanding effortless digital convenience, including delivery.

▷ Elevating the brand, including running better stores.

▸ Competitive data, which might include items such as:

▷ Starbucks still dominates market share.

▷ Consumer choice has exploded since Starbucks elevated the prominence of the coffee shop; myriad competitors are going after Starbucks's traditional retail business and their packaged coffee business.

▷ Starbucks's positioning is built around the combination of breadth of customizable product offering, environmental and sustainability practices, and the in-store experience.

FRONT STAGE		
Customer	Audience profiles	
	Decision-making processes	
Competitive	Expectation setting	
Context	Trends	
	Movements	
BACKSTAGE		
Corporate	Strategy	
	Customer focus	
	Geographic focus	
	Product focus	
	Profit factors	
Brand	USP/value Proposition	
	Positioning	
	Brand growth factors	
	Acquisition/ loyalty factors	
CX	Business requirements	
	Goals/objectives	

Figure 5.3: CX Analysis Map

Leverage	Overcome
Brand strengths	Brand weaknesses
Experience strengths	Experience weaknesses
Weaknesses	Strengths
Trends	Trends
Movements	Movements

Leverage	Overcome
Strengths	Weaknesses
Assets	Liabilities
Strengths	Weaknesses
Assets	Liabilities
Strengths	Weaknesses
Assets	Liabilities

- Context data, which might include items such as:

  ▷ Coffee and related beverage sales are on the rise and are forecasted to remain so.
  ▷ Continued interest in environment and sustainability.
  ▷ Work-from-home policies may strengthen the need for "a third place."

Armed with the aforementioned information, what would make sense as a CX strategy? For the purposes of this example, let's identify three. Keep in mind this is hypothetical and in the spirit of brainstorming; we do not work with Starbucks and have no insider knowledge of the realities of their business and operations.

1. Emotional-oriented strategy: Instill a renewed sense of romanticism about the coffee experience. Resist the gravitational pull toward the transactional (digital as a replacement for human interaction, price competition, speed of service, etc.).

2. Functional-oriented strategy: Build a consistent, reliable, predictable experience that knows the customer and their preferences across all interactions: store formats (e.g., traditional store, pickup only), delivery, and digital channels.

3. Outcomes-oriented strategy: Focus on enabling customer outcomes, whatever those may be. Third place for work or study? Make sure the stores are overly equipped with comfortable seats and charging stations. Decompress and clear the mind? Create a more

serene environment and offer relevant consumable nonfood/beverage items.

With real information and data, more options can be created, but bound by customer data, corporate strategy, and other inputs, realistically we don't need to identify lots of options to choose from. A few tier one choices should reveal themselves if the analysis of the Four C's has been done correctly. From there, we can select the CX Strategy that makes the most sense.

These three completely hypothetical strategic options derive from our framework that serves as a starting point for thinking about the strategic directions and options (Figure 5.4):

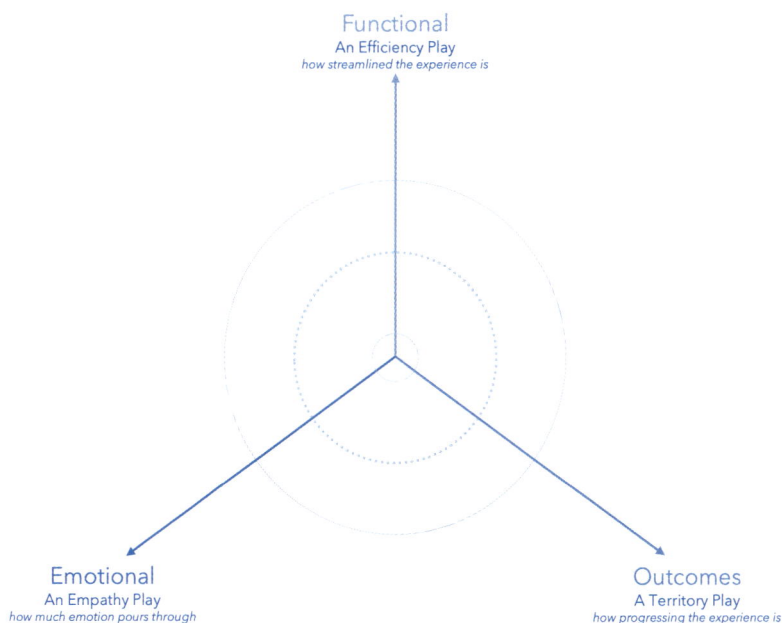

Figure 5.4: CX Strategic Directions

This framework does not mean there are only three choices for a CX strategy. Rather, this identifies areas of exploration. More often than not, elements of all three will exist within the CX strategy. But there has to be one paramount element of the CX strategy, that which the entire CX endeavor maps and supports.

Develop

The process of honing and finalizing the strategy is critically important. Relish this part of the process. Strategy development requires space and time to debate, torture test, and clarify. There are going to be multiple viable options. In the development process, you need to pick just one. It doesn't have to be one from the Explore phase; it can be a blend of Explore phase components.

A few handy criteria help determine whether or not the organization has pushed itself hard enough on the development of a clear, focused, achievable strategy:

- *Specific.* Does it make hard trade-off choices? Are there numerous things you could do that aren't captured in the strategy?
- *Simple.* Is it easy to understand and convey? Can you explain it in fifteen seconds?
- *Actionable.* Does it articulate what the organization is going to go do? Can people picture how they can take action in support of the strategy?

The strategy development process and the strategy process itself do not need to be overengineered and overcomplicated. What's most important is that the right people are involved, the right factors have been assessed, and when you look at the strategy, it feels right for the company and right for the customer. It can always be refined later. The point is to select a strategy that enough people can get behind and then just go.

When organizations have nailed it—when they have a CX strategy that's special—you can see it and feel it:

▶ Its essence can be conveyed simply, and it's easily understood.
▶ It serves to regularly stimulate amazing and often challenging discussions.
▶ It's readily referenced, printed, and hanging on walls.
▶ Experiences begin to form in new places in new ways.
▶ The end-to-end experience becomes stitched together.

CX strategy in the way we strive for is very real, very tangible, and very effective. Far from the cynics' view of strategy, it is essential to successful CX at scale.

BEFORE & AFTER

Before Strategy: Rudderless

A CPG client was continuously pursuing disparate initiatives. Employees frequently executed them in parallel, often over-lapping or conflicting with one another, and had no awareness of the existence of other initiatives. This resulted in customer experiences that were disconnected, duplicative, inconsistent, and full of gaps. There was nothing in place to guide, align, or coordinate these initiatives and no process to harness their collective potential.

After Strategy: Aligned

By adopting a CX strategy, our client was able to provide the guidance needed for teams who never came in contact with one another to pursue the right initiatives that were aligned with one another, resulting in a seamless, consistent customer experience.

Key Points Recap

▶ A CX strategy fills a critical need for CX Champions that corporate and brand strategies do not address: how the experience will feel for customers consistently across the end-to-end customer experience.

▶ Defining a winning CX strategy must be based on a critical analysis on those dynamics—and only those dynamics—that matter for the CX strategy (i.e., don't get caught up in considering dynamics that are already addressed by other strategies or that you shouldn't be solving in CX work).

▶ CX strategy development is a great opportunity to use the process as a way to facilitate collaboration, agreement, and buy-in for ongoing CX execution.

Once a CX strategy is developed, teams can begin to be more intentional and precise in experience design, beginning with CX blueprints.

CHAPTER 6 OVERVIEW

TOPIC PREVIEW

- ▸ A customer experience blueprint (CEB) represents the transition from preparation mode to action mode

- ▸ CEBs specify the future-state customer experience at some future point in time for part—or all—of the customer experience lifecycle

- ▸ The CEB development process is just as valuable as the artifact itself: It builds new bridges across the organization in the name of the customer experience and company profitability.

What we mean by **BLUEPRINT**

Any representation of the future state experience to be built so that teams can clearly understand what they need to create for the customer.

Why **BLUEPRINTS** *are important*

Blueprinting essentially actions against the CX strategy, so it is the connection point between strategy and execution. It's the logical extension of the strategy, setting the stage for execution.

With **BLUEPRINTS...**

Experiences are created according to a rich, visual specification mapped to customers' longitudinal perspective.

Without **BLUEPRINTS...**

Experiences are created to some set of criteria but often result in experience gaps and inconsistencies.

6

STRATEGIC PRACTICE THREE: BLUEPRINTS

*Purposeful Architecture
of Great Experiences*

Blueprinting is the process of envisioning, architecting, and specifying an integrated customer-back experience. "Customer-back" means starting with the customer perspective and determining from there what the company will do to deliver the appropriate experience for the customer. "Integrated" means the experience flows naturally from a given customer's longitudinal perspective and that it brings together various company resources to deliver the experience.

Blueprinting is the conversion point from strategy and planning to execution and change. In the blueprinting process, CX teams develop the desired future state experience for customers, not so far out that it's not feasible or realistic but not so close in that it doesn't require internal evolution and betterment to execute to customer expectations. Accordingly, achieving the vision set forth by the blueprint will require road mapping or phasing of the work to be done. It will require teams to prioritize efforts and associated investments.

As with all plans and roadmaps, blueprints are meant to be flexible. Market conditions change. Customer expectations change. Products change. Companies test and learn. But with the blueprint architecture in place, CX teams have a modular, adaptive, flexible framework within which to make changes as necessary over time.

Blueprint Characteristics

There is a tremendous amount of formalized practices in this space—mature practices that bring the envisioned experience to life. For instance, service design is a very robust and specific skill set that has its own community of experts and trusted methods. There are user flows, process design, and lots of other practices fall under the category of what we refer to as the customer experience blueprint (CEB).

The key mandate here is that organizations must start with the customer in mind and then lay out a desired future state experience that harmonizes customer needs with company interests and that supports the CX strategy. We use the term "blueprint" broadly to refer to any customer-oriented framework that helps envision, shape, and define the desired future state customer experience—that which the customer will see. But our strong preference is for the type of blueprint that is visual in nature and maps to a customer experience view.

Like CEMs and CX strategy, blueprints can exist on a spectrum of altitudes. On the most zoomed-out end of the spectrum, CX Practitioners can look at the entirety of the end-to-end customer experience and how the organization's functional coverage and key processes and programs overlay the customer experience. On the most zoomed-in end of the spectrum, CX Practitioners can specify how the people, content, channels, and other resources will be choreographed to deliver specific experiences for the customer. As long as you're envisioning the experience through the lens of the customer (as discussed in the previous chapter), you're blueprinting.

A CEB describes and visualizes what the experience will be for the customer. It allows CX Practitioners to be thoughtful, purposeful, intentional, and precise in experience development. It also allows everyone involved to define and look at the same future state experience to build toward.

A CEB also identifies the backstage resources that will play a role in experience delivery. That includes technology, data, teams, content, processes, programs, and channels.

Customer at the Center

You can think of a blueprint as representing a single customer's perspective of how he or she would go through the experience in real life. That single customer is representative of all customers or a segment of customers. Consider how they search for the product, buy the product, receive the product, use the product, break the product, find a fix for the product, use the product again differently, call customer service, buy more of the product, watch a YouTube video on the product, etc. Companies use blueprints to architect the answer to that longitudinal customer experience and its associated needs and expectations.

The customer needs to be in the room (figuratively, although customer participation in design sessions is always welcome). The customer needs to be at the center of your work. That means talking about the customer throughout the CX creation process and carefully considering where she is in her customer lifecycle, her profile data, and what she's likely to need next. (Pro tip: Would you be proud or embarrassed to have your customer in the room in any given meeting? That's a great indicator of how authentically customer-centric your organization is.)

Like CEMs, there are many ways for blueprints to be represented (see Figure 6.1 for a more detailed example). Typical blueprint dimensions include:

- ▶ *Front stage.* Envision the future state—what the customer will see. This could be focused on improvements to the existing experience, new experiences close to the current experience, or innovative experiences that are transformative in nature.
- ▶ *Backstage.* Again, envision the future state but related to all of the internal resources we will be bringing together to deliver the envisioned front stage experience. This helps inform the changes or investments required to enable the future state.

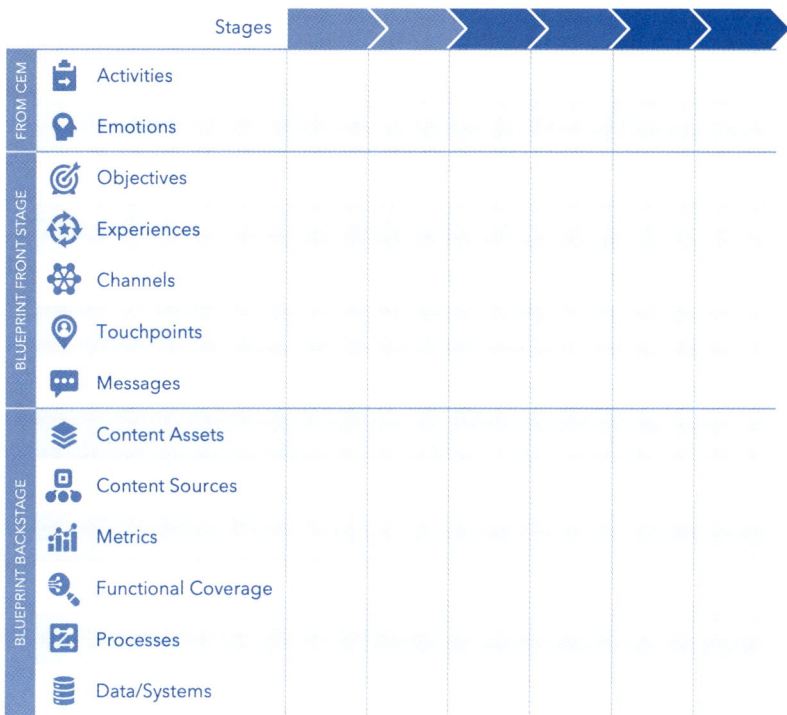

Figure 6.1: Blueprint Structure

To a certain extent, the blueprint sets aside the complexities associated with delivering the current experience, all of the habits and practices that have been built up, all of the silos, and all of the protectionist tendencies that—let's face it—are a reality in every organization. In blueprinting, CX Practitioners can skip over all of that and ask themselves: What would a great experience be for the customer that simultaneously brings to life the CX strategy? A great yet realistically achievable experience? Remember, blueprinting is about defining the future state experience with specificity.

Why take the time to build a blueprint? Why not just go and start fixing experiences? Because everyone has their own ideas on what a better experience could be or what work they want to do or be connected to. Generally they have good intent but sometimes not. A blueprint provides the vehicle (the artifact) and the process (cross-functional collaboration) required to get everyone on the same page, looking at the same problems in the same way, and find solutions that make sense. Like a ransom note that is made up of letters of different sizes, fonts, and colors, without a blueprint, we risk creating a collection of experiences that don't elegantly flow together nor cover the entirety of the CX territory in which we have chosen to play.

We are all familiar with these types of experiences that feel like one company through digital and another company on the phone or in a store or in a sales meeting. We also know about experiences where efforts are duplicated by multiple people or functional areas (like the famous true story of a big software company unwittingly sending fourteen technology salespeople to the same sales pitch without any of them knowing in advance). And we have all experienced gaps where nothing is being offered in a critical moment of need (or a critical moment of opportunity for the company to derive value).

A lot of enterprise-wide CX work is making sure the end-to-end customer perspective overrides internal silo-based perspectives and snaps to the customer perspective.

How We Handle the Product

Because we include the product itself within the totality of the definition of customer experience, we also include the product in the CX blueprint. We, of course, include aspects surrounding the product as well (e.g., buying, learning, building proficiency, help). We include the product, but we don't get to the product feature level because the use cases can be too numerous. A blueprint simply can't accommodate all combinations of software features, theme park rides, or health care visits. It can't accommodate all combinations because a blueprint is meant to lay out an integrated experience that can be actioned, and it would simply be too cumbersome, dense, and confusing to work with if a single blueprint contained myriad product use cases.

As far as using blueprints to drive actual product development, we recommend leaving that to the already well-established and mature product development and operationalization methodologies. From a blueprinting perspective, we tend to leave product development in the hands of product teams to design, develop, and improve the product. But from an insights perspective, you should always be working to feed insights to product development teams on emerging or unmet customer needs, feature requests, etc.

CX Practitioners can include connection to and through the product in a variety of ways, for example:

▶ *Generalized*. For products with expansive, long-tail feature sets like software, where you can't reference the product too deeply without alienating the other use cases.

- *Specific.* For products like buying a home where the process is fairly homogeneous no matter what the scenario.

The blueprinting tool is great at aligning cross-functional CX practices and execution; it is inclusive of product, without the technical and complex nature of the product inhibiting forward progress.

Consider a generalized health care blueprint as an example. CX Practitioners can include physician diagnosis and treatment as well as understanding treatment after the medical visit, treatment compliance, and follow-up scheduling, but not at the specific ailment level. A specific health care blueprint, on the other hand, may be built for, say, knee replacement surgery and get more specific about how that specific experience should play out. Similarly, for a generalized software blueprint, CX Practitioners can include installation and use but not specific feature usage, whereas for a specific software blueprint, CX Practitioners may get into the more unique dynamics around installation and use. You can accommodate the product and weave it into the blueprint without blueprinting the actual product itself.

Like CEMs, blueprints can be done at the enterprise level or the component level:

- *Enterprise.* When companies want to blueprint the totality of the end-to-end customer experience, an enterprise blueprint can be developed, with the enterprise CEMs serving as the context and anchor. An enterprise blueprint focuses on general front stage experiences across the end-to-end customer experience; it does not get into the detail of the experience because that would be too dense and unwieldy—that's what component blueprints are for. Enterprise blueprints are great for seeing the big picture, understanding the high-level flow of the experience, and for helping the company determine if it wants to address parts of the customer experience that it traditionally has not supported (for instance, should the company address earlier-stage experiences, like enterprise software companies do by putting software in the hands of students years before they may or may not influence a software purchase? Should the company do more to help customers be successful post-purchase, like automakers do with customer education?). This type of blueprint also may identify new ways of handling functional coverage (i.e., which internal team handles which component of the experience) as well as map the backstage resources to enable experiences, further identifying new ways of supporting different aspects of the experience (e.g., data sources, systems). While not execution-ready, enterprise blueprints do spark action backstage by identifying things to pursue backstage.

▶ *Component.* Like component CEMs, component blueprints zoom into some subset of the end-to-end customer experience. This could be at the stage level, like post-purchase and ongoing use. It could be for a specific set of customer activities. It could be in a specific channel or a specific customer segment. Component blueprints get much more detailed and are much more requirements oriented. They are highly prescriptive.

Process for Developing a CX Blueprint

As is the case with all of our frameworks, blueprinting is both a process and a deliverable.

Developing the blueprint requires cross-functional collaboration and cooperation. Going through the blueprinting process is a great way to create new cross-functional relationships, learn more about what others do in the organization, and, most importantly, it's an opportunity to develop trust among the parties involved. The blueprinting process will likely identify new experiences that need to be created, so new personal connections may need to be made.

The process will also likely identify areas of overlap and duplication, which suggests that someone or some team may need to lose some of what they do. That's clearly a threat to their very existence, and people will hold on for dear life. Every organization will have a different way of dealing with those circumstances (e.g., shared KPIs, role definition), but fear and anxiety need to be minimized as much as possible. It can't be eliminated—blueprinting can represent something new and exciting but also something new and scary. It's often unchartered territory. But the courage and appetite for change comes a bit more easily when it's under the banner of improving the customer experience and improving company profitability.

As with other CX efforts, the right people need to be involved. Sales, marketing, digital, product, support, and other teams responsible for client experience delivery must contribute to this effort. Even if the blueprint is for a subset of the customer experience, it's still really helpful to have lateral teams at least aware of the work because all experiences have the opportunity to influence other experiences. For instance, sales and marketing claims influence downstream realization (or not) of expectations. If you're focusing on a post-sale blueprint, customer temperament at that point is likely based on the trajectory set by sales and marketing.

Generally, the steps involved in blueprinting are as follows:

Frame

We begin the process by specifying the blueprint context: All products or a subset? All markets? Which roles/personas? New customers, existing customers, or both? Which stages of the customer lifecycle?

All of these criteria define the parameters of the blueprint. They define the blueprint to be developed.

Prepare

Having determined the scope of the blueprint, it's time to pull together the inputs and frameworks that will inform the blueprint. The blueprint must be rooted in customer insights and in internal resources and capabilities. We recommend the following as a blueprint foundation (Note: We use Excel for this because we can separate information into separate tabs, but PowerPoint works as well):

▸ **Overview.** The parameters established by the Frame process should be the starting point as well as objectives for the blueprint—both customer-facing (i.e., product success) and internally-facing (e.g., increased ninety-day retention).

- ▶ **Personas:** Because the blueprint is oriented around the customer, you need to include customer insights in the blueprint framework. We like to pull in audience profile information, ideally personas. It not only makes accessing this information painless (since everyone using the blueprint may not have access to the latest personas), but it further reinforces that you are creating experiences for actual human beings, not abstract objects.

- ▶ **Narrative:** The narrative represents the story of the current state experiences and its positives and negatives as well as the story of what people are thinking, doing, and feeling across the experience. CEMs typically don't include a story, so we find it helpful to weave this into the blueprint. It supercharges the ability to design experiences that move people forward, minimize friction, and create experiences that matter.

- ▶ **CEM.** Whether a CEM already exists or still needs to be developed, the CEM is instrumental in a) serving as the context for the blueprint and b) identifying what experiences need to be blueprinted. Ultimately CX Practitioners need to identify and catalog existing practices, the extent to which they are still necessary, experience shortcomings and gaps, technology capabilities, software, content, digital properties, etc.—all of the front and backstage components of current state experience delivery. CX Practitioners need to capture and inventory the skills, assets, and capabilities available for leverage. This is critical because CX

Practitioners have to know what they're doing today to determine the gap between current and future states.

Envision

With a deep understanding of customers' needs, expectations, and behaviors, you are ready to envision the end-to-end, longitudinal experience (again, end-to-end refers to the CEM stage[s] the blueprint is meant to address).

Here, CX Practitioners can think as broadly and creatively as the blueprint parameters will allow about how various types of content, communications channels, human interaction, digital properties, and physical environments will come together to serve the objectives of the blueprint. It's important to think about how resources will be deployed—when, where, how, who—in service of those objectives.

Architect

Once a broad-strokes definition of the future state experience is in place, CX Practitioners need to further specify the future state experience. This is where we get more specific about engagement cadence, channels, messaging, and other experience attributes, all within the context of the CEM. This is where CX Practitioners need to think about architecting experiences with precision and intention to orchestrate great experiences for customers.

The development of the blueprint provides myriad opportunities to engage, collaborate, learn, and build relationships across the company, all in service of a common goal:

a better customer experience. This work brings together cross-functional initiatives, processes, and teams to snap to the customer experience. The blueprint helps to build new working relationships across teams and identify capabilities that need to be addressed.

Generally, blueprints should include:

- **Front Stage**
  - ▷ Objectives
    - – What the customer is trying to achieve (either per stage or per activity)
    - – What the company is trying to achieve (either per stage or per activity)
  - ▷ Experiences
    - – Typically, experiences represent a set of touch-points (e.g., thought leadership, a welcome series, training, or customer service). There will be time downstream to get very specific about how this will be executed. Here, the idea is to represent various experiences that should play out across the stages and activities being blueprinted.
    - – Think of this as a Gannt chart where experiences can span multiple activities and stages or, vice versa, multiple experiences can support a given activity. The key here is to think about what the customer needs and then architect the company's answer to that need via this experience blueprint.

- ▷ Channels
  - – Where the interactions with the customer will take place: physical environment, website, mobile app, email, phone, etc.
- ▷ Touchpoints
  - – Specific representation of the components within experiences. For example, an email welcome series would identify the number of emails and the purpose of each email.
- ▷ Messages
  - – For each relevant experience or touchpoint, key messages are identified. This isn't customer-facing copy—that happens later. Here the intent is to bring the touchpoints to life by conveying what the company will be saying to the customer generally.
  - – This step includes versioning and personalization (for instance, customers may receive one version of a message while prospects may receive another).
  - – This step also include calls to action (i.e., what the company is asking of the customer).

- ► **Backstage**
  - ▷ Content assets
    - – The various types of content required to support the front stage experience (e.g., video highlight reel, case studies, usage instructions). Some of this content may already exist; some may need to be developed.

▷ Content sources
  – For existing content, indication of where that content resides in internal systems
▷ Metrics
  – Indicators of tactical performance by stage, experience, activity, etc.
▷ Functional Coverage
  – The internal organizational functions that are supporting, enabling, and/or delivering experiences to the customer
▷ Processes
  – The internal processes that are driving customer experiences
▷ Data/Systems
  – Indication of which data sources and/or systems will power experience delivery

CX Initiative Management

Once the blueprint is developed, socialized, and ratified, the blueprint will spawn all sorts of action to refine existing experiences or stand up new experiences or processes to cover experience gaps:

▶ *Program realignment.* Moving items earlier or later or extending or narrowing their focus.
▶ *Program rationalization.* Combining or cutting out duplicated experiences.

- *Process development.* Working together across teams and functions for better handoff processes from team to team, stage to stage.
- *Business requirements.* Tactical-level operationalization requirements.
- *Technology requirements.* Delivering the new experience may require new or modified technology capabilities. This could be new CRM or support software, expanded server capacity, or new uptime requirements.
- *Data requirements.* You may need to unify customer data that is currently spread across multiple databases, capture new data, or cleanse existing data.
- *Content strategy.* The blueprint will likely call for new content, content rationalization, and new ways of providing content.
- *Initiative definition.* New experiences may need to be developed, creating new initiatives that need to get funded, resourced, and executed.

The reality is that all of the CXS and CEB work will be happening in parallel to the routine running of the business. Initiatives are wrapping up, in flight, and being planned. The CEB may specify new initiatives, entering a system that is running vigorously with initiative owners who are not simply going to stand down because of the blueprinting process, at least not because of the blueprinting process alone. Like CX work itself, you need to take the perspective of initiative owners. They fought hard some time ago for funding, their name is attached to the work, and their career stands to gain or not based on this work. Because of the stratified nature of the age, purpose, potential impact, and time horizon of the in-flight and new CX initiatives, we can apply a stratified oversight framework as follows (see Figure 6.2):

- *Follow*. Initiatives where you may not be welcome (it happens). You may not be able to influence it, but you can simply note that the initiative exists and observe and follow its progress.
- *Track*. Initiatives that you can't influence but are plugged into through regular updates so you're kept up to speed.
- *Influence*. Initiatives that you don't control but the owners welcome input and influence to ensure it's on strategy.
- *Own*. Initiatives you as a CX owner control on all decisions.

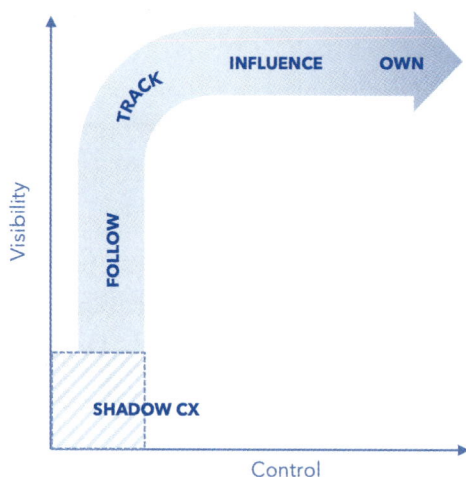

Figure 6.2: CX Initiative Oversight Framework

BEFORE & AFTER

Before Blueprints: Haphazard

With every intention of truly helping customers, a B2B technology client was feverishly producing content, programs, more content, and more programs to help customers as they were trying to use the technology successfully in their companies. Information was hard to wade through, confusing, and filled with dead ends. The information existed in multiple locations. Customers didn't know where to go for help. They felt stuck, frustrated, and on their own, unable to move at the speed they needed and unable to leverage the full value of the technology. This ultimately negatively impacted customer satisfaction, loyalty, and lifetime value.

After Blueprints: Intentional

With blueprints in place, our client was able to begin the process of sunsetting content and programs and instead focus on executing streamlined experience flows that actually moved customers forward with the product. Engagement tools and software were consolidated to enable blueprint execution, increasing efficiency, reducing costs, and eliminating a set of infrastructure and associated administration.

Key Points Recap

▶ The blueprinting process provides a canvas on which you can be thoughtful, purposeful, and intentional in designing experiences that support customer needs and support the CX strategy.

▶ Blueprinting provides a bridge between functional teams and can foster meaningful internal relationships.

▶ Representing both front stage and backstage in blueprints makes the blueprints tangible and connects the blueprints to operations and execution.

With insights, CX strategy, and blueprinting covered, we now turn our attention to more internal organizational critical enablers of CX at scale: the operating model (chapter 7) and culture (chapter 8).

CHAPTER 7 OVERVIEW

TOPIC PREVIEW	▸ Operating models enable the organization to more effectively deliver CX success.
	▸ Operating models are unique to client cultures and ways of working.
	▸ A simple, high-functioning operating model must contain several basic components.
What we mean by **OPERATING MODEL**	Operating model defines a company's approach to delivering its CX strategy, identifying ways of working, shared expectations, and approaches to collectively achieve success.
Why **OPERATING MODEL** *is important*	A clear operating model enables the organization to engage more effectively in the often challenging work of CX. It helps create cooperation, heighten collaborative engagement, streamline execution, and nurture a culture of shared ownership and success.
With **OPERATING MODEL...**	The company has defined ways of working and coordinating efforts across teams and across the enterprise.
Without **OPERATING MODEL...**	Teams are left on their own, working in silos, perhaps doing great but suboptimized work, thus leaving value on the table for the organization.

7

STRATEGIC PRACTICE FOUR: OPERATING MODEL

Wiring the Organization for Success

We think of the CX operating model as an organizational system that ensures the consistent and effective delivery of the CX strategy. Some might call it governance, structures, or key processes; we see it as having attributes of all of these. Our view is that the CX operating model is more of an eco-system akin to the circulatory system to the human body, public transit within a city, or a coral reef in the ocean. Each has its own component parts, organizing models, behaviors, and ways of working that depend on, integrate with, and contribute to the whole. The operating model ultimately allows the organization to function with greater efficiency and alignment and ultimately scale CX success.

At their base, CX operating models define:

- Who is involved: Named individuals and organizations participating in CX
- How they are involved: Roles and responsibilities guiding the engagement of individuals/teams/departments involved in the deliverables or work areas
- Guardrails for how they can work effectively together: Shared standards/policies, decision/approval rights, depth of work, and operating procedures

We know when CX operating models are broken, ill-defined, misunderstood, or, worse, not present. It's easy to spot. You see duplication of efforts. You see business areas engage and disengage at will. You see initiatives drag and stop. You see conflict and friction. And, ultimately, you get a disjointed customer experience. It's like the ransom note we discussed earlier (inconsistent, incongruous experiences) that represents the internal dysfunction of the organization.

There Is No Single Best Practice Model

We wish it were as simple as using a "lift and land" approach for building a CX operating model. However, creating an effective CX operating model requires a customized approach, so there is no universal template. Why does it need to be so tailored?

First, the priorities set by a CX strategy differ across organizations, affecting various parts of the business and necessitating the integration of diverse, preexisting systems.

For example, one organization might need to link a call center model with a digital platform, while another might need to align financial processes with marketing tactics or integrate a customer success program with a rewards platform. These differing needs mean that the operating model must serve as a unique connective framework that not only aligns these disparate components but also guides the seamless delivery of the desired customer experience.

Second, the set of actions required to deliver on a CX strategy will vary significantly depending on the organization's portfolio of CX efforts. The operating model might need to support a mix of sustained long-term initiatives, short-term tactical projects, new pilots, or the planned discontinuation of certain services or experiences. Incidentally, we find one of the most challenging aspects of CX work is determining which elements to phase out or retire while introducing new ones. An effective CX operating model must be tailored to accommodate variations in the CX initiative life stage.

With that in mind, CX operating models are usually shaped by the degree of strategic and operational centralization within an organization. We often observe elements of the following archetypal models (outlined in Table 7.1), though organizations rarely follow them strictly.

MODEL	WORKS BEST FOR
Decentralized: Departments or business units have full autonomy, each handling its own CX efforts.	▸ Large, diverse organizations where departments have distinct customer segments and needs ▸ Ideal for companies with varied product lines or services, allowing each unit to tailor the CX approach to their specific audience ▸ Suits brands that prioritize flexibility and responsiveness to localized market conditions
Matrixed: CX roles and responsibilities are shared across departments, with cross-functional teams collaborating on initiatives.	▸ Organizations that require high levels of collaboration and have interdependent departments ▸ Effective in cultures with mature teamwork and communication practices
Federated: Central oversight guides CX strategy and guidelines while execution is distributed across departments.	▸ Organizations that need a balance between centralized strategy and localized execution ▸ Suitable for companies that want to maintain a unified brand vision while allowing flexibility for departmental or regional adaptation ▸ Works well for brands seeking consistency in customer experience without stifling individual department innovation
Center of Excellence: Specialized teams provide expertise and best practices to support CX initiatives across departments.	▸ Organizations looking to standardize best practices and drive innovation through specialized knowledge ▸ Ideal for companies aiming to lead in CX by leveraging deep expertise and fostering continuous improvement ▸ Suits brands that want to ensure high-quality CX while encouraging departments to adopt proven methodologies

MODEL	WORKS BEST FOR
Centralized: A central team manages and drives all CX efforts across the organization.	▸ Brands that require a single cohesive customer experience across all touchpoints ▸ Companies with a strong central vision and operational leadership, ensuring all CX efforts align closely with overall business objectives

Table 7.1: CX Operating Model Archetypes

We've worked with clients who have run the gamut: those who operationalized CX at an audience level, deployed CX as a shared service, modeled CX as a center of excellence, attached CX to a specific or many lines of business, driven CX by the CEO, or even completely democratized CX to the front line. Some companies have operationalized, or attempted to operationalize, several of these models at the same time. There simply is no one-size-fits-all approach.

What We Like to See in CX Operating Models

We have identified a set of attributes that are critical to creating a CX operating model that works within a given company culture.

Nurtures Broad and Holistic Collaboration

Given the nature and span of experience, it's clear that, short of the CEO, no single department can guide and execute all aspects of experience.

This work is highly cross-functional, perhaps more so than any other practice. It touches so many different parts of the corporate organism to define, prioritize, operationalize, and scale great experiences across the customer experience. From product to customer success to marketing, all departments are involved in various aspects because they bring specific domain expertise, operational capability, and adjacent business goals. This requires more of a Renaissance approach, where diverse experts collaborate like the master craftsmen of the past, each contributing their unique skills and insights. The focus is on integrating this range of expertise through purposeful and structured collaboration, with robust frameworks in place to encourage effective, positive teamwork across varied groups.

Accommodates Ever-Shifting Participation

A great model readily accommodates changing engagement. People come and go, corporate plans shift, organizations restructure, and outside partners and subject matter experts (SMEs) are brought in. A great model accommodates this fluidity, enabling people to move in and out and perhaps back again. These models offer transparency with clear and easily accessible expectations for participation. They include mechanisms for shadowing and onboarding/offboarding new members as well as maintaining connections with past participants through ongoing communications.

Balances a Tight and Loose Approach

Great models expertly balance both tight and loose elements. They implement tight characteristics—such as well-defined participation, consistent routines, focused shared processes, and clear decision-making authority—when maintaining consistency and alignment is crucial. Simultaneously, they embrace loose, flexible aspects that prioritize intention over rigid rules, guided by principles, and empower dynamic, decentralized decision-making where adaptability is needed. This overall approach enables organizations to uphold consistency where it's most important while remaining agile and responsive in areas that benefit from more flexibility.

Emphasizes Clear, Easy-to-Understand Processes

We love processes that are simple and easy to understand. While documentation is necessary, the best models are straightforward and intuitive, making them easy to follow. In many cases, these processes are visual or can fit on a single page, pared down to the essential information that people need to know and comply with. This simplicity makes them easy to share and adopt across the organization, ensuring everyone can engage with them effectively without feeling overwhelmed. Where appropriate, sharing those processes attached to customer stories and "what exceptional looks like" can be powerful. It brings to life how the implementation and adoption of process improves customers' lives.

Intentionally Managed

Someone must always have their eyes and ears on the model, assessing, diagnosing, and identifying issues and opportunities for improvement. This individual (or individuals) grounds participants in the operating model expectations and frameworks to ensure effectiveness. This also helps to establish a degree of accountability for the model's success.

Designed for Iteration

Great CX operating models are designed to change. They are always considered works in progress, evolving as organizations gain more experience and mature their CX domains. Ideally, they start with a basic CX operating model and deepen and expand as needed, reflecting the ongoing growth and development of the organization.

Next, we'll share a basic operating model that can be adapted and evolved based on the needs of the organization.

A Simplified CX Operating Model

In this section, we present a pro forma for a simplified CX operating model aimed at streamlining and improving how organizations manage customer interactions. While a complete CX operating model would be based on a comprehensive audit of needs, this starting point offers a straightforward framework that integrates leadership, strategy, execution, and coordination to create a more unified approach to CX initiatives. It includes what we have seen to be the core components for success—a defined structure, shared processes, and a clear charter. By adopting this or similar streamlined models, organizations can enhance cross-functional collaboration, minimize complexity, and ensure that all customer experience efforts are aligned with their strategic objectives.

Organizes and Guides Clear Participation

When designing the operating model, aim for a lean, easy to understand structure that accommodates broad cross-functional participation and effective management of customer experience initiatives. We identify four critical and distinct structurally related domains of participation that are central to success: leadership, steering, execution, and coordination. Each of these domains is crucial and requires diverse, explicit participation and interactions between various stakeholders (Figure 7.1).

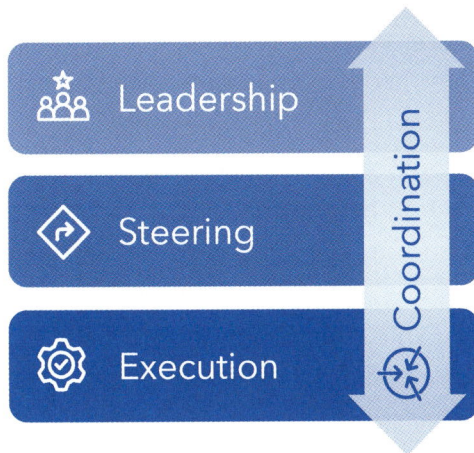

Figure 7.1: Domains of Participation

- Leadership: Ensuring alignment to overall business priorities and key strategies
- Steering: Forming the strategic direction and guiding the organization in its CX work
- Execution: Delivering experience initiatives with alignment, accountability, and recognition elements
- Coordination: Ensuring effective management and integration of the domains

The goal should be to cultivate, activate, and manage the model as a cohesive and inclusive community. This collective approach ensures that everyone involved understands their role and how it connects to the broader CX strategy.

This structure serves as the foundation, with individuals and groups moving in and out based on the specific needs of the work, a CX project's lifecycle, and the collective maturity. Understanding this dynamic allows us to think more effectively about the roles within this system and how they interconnect rather than operate in silos. For instance, leadership must ensure that all CX initiatives are aligned with the organization's strategic goals while steering committees provide direction and guidance. The execution teams are responsible for implementing these initiatives with a focus on accountability, and coordination ensures that all efforts are integrated and managed efficiently.

With top-level domains mapped, detailed responsibilities and ideal participant criteria are defined (Table 7.2). These serve to more effectively identify, recruit, and engage the right mix of organizational stakeholders in CX work.

LEADERSHIP

Participants

C-suite / board leaders charged with organizational direction and strategic accountability. With broad operational responsibilities and backgrounds, their perspectives toward CX and its relative value will vary significantly.

Responsibilities

- ▶ Setting organizational strategy and vision
- ▶ Stewarding and overseeing financial health and resources
- ▶ Positioning resources to support strategic initiatives
- ▶ Ensuring alignment and integration of CX to governance models, operating plans, and incentive structures
- ▶ High-level CX decision-making and program sponsorship
- ▶ Nurturing CX vision and culture across the organization

STEERING

Participants

Cross-functional leader champions with a vested interest in transformational CX success. They excel at strategy setting, are recognized as leaders organization-wide, bring diverse perspectives, and have varied CX experience. Typically reporting to the C-suite, they manage expectations and unite others to drive change.

Responsibilities

- ▶ Develop and maintain a comprehensive CX strategy
- ▶ Prioritize CX efforts with the greatest strategic impact
- ▶ Establish clear success metrics and KPIs
- ▶ Activate and sponsor key cross-functional work teams
- ▶ Plan and advocate for adequate resources for CX initiatives
- ▶ Communicate progress to senior leadership
- ▶ Promote a customer-centric culture
- ▶ Risk planning and mitigation

EXECUTION

Participants	This diverse group executes CX programs and tactics, typically as functional subject matter and domain experts. Embedded within operations or at the corporate level, they deliver myriad CX initiatives across the organization. Known for their expert collaboration and relationship-building skills, these practitioners ensure the successful implementation of CX strategies.
Responsibilities	▸ Provide CX-level tactical oversight and delivery ▸ Analyze data and discern insights/signals ▸ Offer consultative guidance and apply best practices ▸ Conduct training, education, and coaching ▸ Facilitate employee recognition programs ▸ Implement CX initiatives and programs ▸ Reporting and guidance to Steering leads

COORDINATION

Participants	Coordination, aka program management, oversees the integration and management of CX efforts. They ensure effective coordination of initiatives and activities within and across domains. Skilled in process management and communication, they maintain alignment, track progress, and facilitate smooth execution of CX strategies.
Responsibilities	▸ Provide program and change management support ▸ Ensure comprehensive communication strategies ▸ Act as the backbone of CX program management, holding initiatives together ▸ Conduct stage gate reviews ▸ Facilitate the adoption of shared processes ▸ Manage charters

Table 7.2: Domains of Participation Detail

Has Defined Key Processes

Defining common shared processes is crucial for the success of a CX operating model. These processes enable consistent, high-quality interactions with customers across various touchpoints and ensure that the CX strategy aligns with the organization's goals. They reduce confusion and potential conflict by creating shared expectations and streamlining internal engagement. This fosters a collaborative, trusted environment where everyone works more effectively toward the same objectives. The standard processes we try to define in any operating model include:

▶ Decision-Making Frameworks—Establish processes for making decisions, including criteria, involved parties, and escalation paths to resolve service defects and issues efficiently.

▶ Portfolio Management Models—Ensure alignment with strategy and allow for ongoing management of the optimal mix of CX activities across the enterprise.

▶ Project Management Standards—Share methods for chartering, planning, executing, and reviewing projects. This includes setting timelines, milestones, and deliverables to keep work on track.

▶ Meeting and Reporting Rhythms—Establish a regular schedule for meetings (daily stand-ups, weekly reviews, etc.) and reporting to maintain transparency and accountability.

▶ Document and Knowledge Sharing—Create a centralized repository for stories, documents, guidelines, and best practices to facilitate knowledge sharing and continuity.

- ▸ Communication Plans—Set clear channels and norms for communication within the workgroup and with external stakeholders to ensure efficient information exchange.
- ▸ Onboarding and Training Procedures—Standardize onboarding for new team members and ongoing training programs to ensure everyone is equipped with the necessary skills and knowledge.

To support these processes, it is important to document in simple and scalable procedures that ensure clarity and transparency across all activities. This approach not only enhances efficiency but also promotes a unified understanding of objectives and methods, which is crucial for the successful implementation of a CX operating model.

Is Documented and Managed via a Charter

A charter is a foundational document that establishes the framework for how the CX team operates. It defines the team's purpose, practices, and goals, ensuring that all efforts align with the strategic approach to delivering the CX strategy.

The charter is crucial because it provides a shared understanding and focus, eliminating the need for team members to guess or fill in the blanks about their roles and tasks. By specifying team roles and key processes, it reduces confusion and enhances efficiency, preventing potential conflicts and overlaps in responsibilities. Additionally, the charter sets clear expectations for success, aligning the team's work with the company's customer experience strategy. It further helps measure progress and ensure accountability. The key components of the charter are:

▸ Mission and Vision: Outlines the team's overarching goals and the desired impact on customer experience. This section should articulate the long-term aspirations and the core purpose of the CX team. These are informed by the CX strategy.

▸ Objectives and Performance Metrics: Details specific goals the team aims to achieve and the metrics for measuring success. These objectives should be SMART (specific, measurable, achievable, relevant, and time-bound) to provide clear targets and accountability. These are also informed by the CX strategy.

▸ Team Roles and Responsibilities: Defines the specific roles within the CX team, including who is responsible for what tasks and how they interact with each other. This section ensures everyone knows their duties and how they contribute to the overall goals.

▸ Key Processes and Practices: Describes the essential processes and practices the team will follow to achieve their objectives. This can include methodologies for project management, communication plans, meeting cadences, and other critical activities.

▸ Review and Adaptation: Sets up a plan for regularly reviewing and updating the charter to reflect changes in the business environment, customer needs, or team dynamics. This ensures the charter remains relevant and effective over time.

By creating a detailed and well-thought-out charter, the team can operate with clear direction and purpose, ensuring that all efforts contribute to the overarching goal of enhancing customer experience. This foundational document not only guides daily operations but also mitigates potential scope creep and aligns the team's work with the broader strategic vision of the organization.

BEFORE & AFTER

Before Operating Model: Ad Hoc

A client in the communications industry operated in traditional customer-facing silos: marketing, sales, customer success, and customer support. Each department created customer experiences, often without recognizing them as such. Campaigns, sales interactions, and support calls were part of the customer experience but disjointed. Teams—not leadership—first recognized the importance of a seamless, cohesive customer experience and noticed the disconnects as customers moved from one silo to another. As they pursued a more holistic CX design, it became evident that they needed a defined operating model. The lack of a formal, cross-functional way of working for CX efforts hindered cooperation and coordination. To be successful, they needed to establish a clear CX operating model that would provide the framework for seamless execution, align efforts across departments, and ensure a unified approach to customer experience.

After Operating Model: Formalized

Recognizing the need for a defined CX operating model, our communications client chose to implement a center of excellence (CoE) model to leverage deep expertise and standardize best practices. After conducting an audit, they identified key shared common goals through diversely applied practice areas such as experience research, design, data analytics, and process improvement. They established a specialized central team dedicated to deploying those capabilities with consistency, breaking down silos and integrating efforts across marketing, sales, customer success, and customer support. Over the course of several years, implementing the model contributed to a 25 percent overall increase in customer satisfaction scores, proving the value of a well-defined CX operating model.

Key Points Recap

▸ There is no one-size-fits-all approach; CX operating models must be customized to fit unique organizational needs and priorities.

▸ Effective models will foster collaboration, balance centralization, and use lean, intuitive processes.

▸ Models should be designed to evolve, continuously improving as the organization grows and learns.

Now you've got a framework for an explicit CX operating model. It lays the pipes and wiring that will allow the work to flow better through the organization. Now let's move on to the critical role of creating a culture of CX.

CHAPTER 8 OVERVIEW

TOPIC PREVIEW	▸ CX needs to be seen as amplifying the existing attributes of company culture.
	▸ A culture will always hold diverse attitudes toward CX; it is not monolithic.
	▸ Nurturing a positive culture that embraces CX takes real, intentional work.
What we mean by **CULTURE**	A CX culture refers to an organizational mindset and environment where decisions and actions are driven by the goal of improving the customer's experience.
Why **CULTURE** *is important*	An aligned CX culture creates the institutional understanding, conviction, and practices necessary to create breakthrough customer experiences at scale over time.
With **CULTURE...**	The organization inherently embraces an orientation toward the customer—an external versus internal focus.
Without **CULTURE...**	CX Champions are fighting uphill for attention and engagement in CX efforts.

8

STRATEGIC PRACTICE FIVE: CULTURE

Organizational Engagement and
Nurturing a Culture of CX

You may want to skip this chapter. Don't. It's of critical importance. It is the red thread that will, more than any other aspect of experience, determine whether CX is a permanent shift in the way of the business or if it's a short-term tactic. You've heard the phrase "culture eats strategy for breakfast." It's true.

Customer experience is a direct reflection of an organization's culture, revealing both its strengths and weaknesses. It mirrors the values and behaviors ingrained within an organization, shaping how teams approach their work. To deliver great customer experiences at scale over time, teams have to understand and internalize the importance of customer experience. They have to inherently feel like the organization is moving in the right direction on CX. Otherwise, they won't adopt it or bring it into their everyday work. If they understand and believe in the company's approach to CX, then organizations can arm them with the tools, practices, and methodologies that will help them to be successful with experience delivery.

But it's more than just the front line, the people who touch the customers—the call center employees, gate agents, or baristas. In fact, in our experience, the people who actually interact with customers every day are the ones who understand and believe in the principles of CX more than those who don't. They may not recognize it as CX or use this language, but they know it inherently. They get the backlash from the broken experiences. They see firsthand when their organizations fail the customer or when lack of an enterprise approach to CX creates unnecessary roadblocks. Unfortunately, executive and operational leadership can be a greater hindrance to the success of CX than the front line itself. Ultimately, culture work is about ensuring that everyone—from top to bottom—knows and believes they have a role to play and that they, together, are empowered to take action.

So creating and nurturing broad cultural advocacy is a key never-ending responsibility for CX Champions. If you want to do this at scale over time, your culture has to be aligned to experience efforts. Full stop. Period.

Let's look at some of the keys to successful culture development and tools that can be applied.

Identify the CX Values

We don't even like to raise the specter of change as it relates to having a culture of CX. Change raises fear of the unknown, aversion to loss, and perceived dissonance with current beliefs. There's no better way to kill CX than to attach it to changing a culture.

In fact, changing culture has never been our intent with any of the work we've done with clients. It's much more about reconnecting and reawakening the aspects of customer experience that were always there. No client or known brand would have been successful had they not delivered superb customer experience at some time in their existence. The issue is that they've lost their customer centricity, or perhaps it's simply dormant, lying in wait to be reawakened. Perhaps they are so big that they overindexed on supporting massive, complex operations. Growth requires scale in all aspects of capability. But as the growth occurs, the inherent day-one connection to the customer gets lost. It's not that it's gone or never existed; it's simply an unworked or forgotten muscle. In any case, it certainly isn't about change. It's about tapping into the DNA of the organization.

Therefore, seek to find those living aspects your company's culture—and there are always many—that are serving customer experience well. It's already rooted in the culture of every organization we've worked with. The job is to frame CX as a practice, which is, again, already being done by an organization that aligns with and ultimately amplifies those aspects of culture. Emphasize that CX *strengthens* an organizational culture; CX does not *change* it.

In doing CX work, start with a clear-eyed look for and

at aspects of the organization that set direction and organizational ethos or culture. Then work to frame the strategic intent and direction of CX in support of those culture drivers, for instance:

- *Values.* Values represent the core principles that guide behavior and decision-making within the organization. By aligning CX efforts with the core values of the organization, CX Practitioners can ensure that customer experience is a natural extension of what the company stands for. When employees see that CX efforts are rooted in their shared values, they are more likely to embrace and champion these initiatives.

  ▷ For example, if the company has "boldness" as one of its values, that gives CX Champions permission to aggressively advocate for CX. It suggests a safe environment within which to bring up radical change.

- *Employee Engagement.* Employee engagement represents programs that address key areas of employee motivation. It is crucial for a thriving CX culture. Engaged employees are more likely to deliver outstanding customer service. CX Champions can work to integrate CX training and recognition programs that motivate employees by showing them the direct impact of their efforts on customer satisfaction and business success.

  ▷ ANA, Japan's All Nippon Airways, holds an annual "Omotenashi Professional Contest" to recognize and celebrate teams that provide exceptional service and embody the Japanese spirit of *omotenashi*—whole-hearted hospitality. For example, a recent winning team developed custom welcome kits tailored to different passenger segments, such as children, business travelers, or elderly passengers, enhancing the flight experience with thoughtful, personalized touches. By emphasizing such innovative practices, ANA motivates employees to excel, boosts morale, and aligns team efforts with business success, fostering a culture of dedication and experience excellence.

▶ *Stories and Legends.* Stories and legends—narratives about the organization's history and key figures that shape the corporate identity—are potent tools for embedding CX into the organizational culture. Sharing success stories of employees who have gone above and beyond for customers can inspire others and reinforce the value of a customer-centric approach. These narratives become part of the corporate lore, promoting a culture that values and rewards exceptional customer experience.

▷ One prominent health care client frequently shares a story among employees that illustrates the dedication of one of the founders, who was directly involved in the construction and operation of the facilities she founded in the mid-1800s. This particular founder was known for her hands-on approach. She often supervised construction sites and participated in physical labor and was famously seen with a hammer in hand, ready to assist and ensure every detail met the highest standards to serve the community's needs. This story exemplifies leadership, perseverance, and dedication, forming the foundation for the organization's commitment to compassionate care. The implication for customer experience (CX) is clear: This narrative reinforces the importance of leading by example and fostering a supportive leader culture, reminding leaders and employees that empathy, resourcefulness, and active involvement are crucial to delivering exceptional customer experiences.

Also spend time understanding less explicit but equally important drivers of culture such as leadership styles, power structures, and workplace norms. But for these explicit culture drivers, we like to use a formal tool to capture the essentials: a values assessment (Figure 8.1).

Now there is a robust inventory and assessment of collective drivers of culture. This allows you to explicitly map how and where improved CX relates to and can amplify these drivers of the *existing* culture. Ultimately these become ingredients that you can infuse in culture efforts.

Know the CX Mindsets

In a magical world, CX Champions would have a conversation with every person at a company to truly understand their perspective on the world of CX. Many won't know what CX means, and this is a perspective as well. Many will be completely indifferent. Others will embrace the idea. Several will actively reject the implications of CX. But ideally, you would be able to sit down with them and understand their world, their concerns, and their unique perspectives, then engage in a thoughtful, constructive dialogue about CX. And, over time, hopefully, you will be able to hear them out and demonstrate how CX can help and win them over.

But, of course, talking to everyone is impossible. That said, it should be your conceptual intent. Meet people where they are by understanding their perspectives or lack thereof. By knowing their perspective, you can start to engage with them and nurture a positive CX culture.

So how can CX Champions get their arms around this dynamic in a systematic and actionable way? We like to think about two dimensions: role and disposition.

Role

We'll start with role, a more straightforward and familiar construct. For the purposes of culture development efforts, we tend to think about three key roles that ultimately drive the outcomes and success of CX.

▸ **Leadership:** The leadership layer comprises the top executives and managers who set the strategic direction and overall vision for the organization. For example: the CEO, the CFO, the board of directors.

▸ **Operations:** The operations layer involves the middle management and support staff who oversee the implementation of strategies, manage resources, and ensure

Align

CULTURE MAP

Values	
Mission and Vision	
Employee Engagement	
Stories and Legends	

Figure 8.1: CX Values Assessment

Leverage   **Overcome**

efficient workflows. For example: the HR group, a product division, the marketing department.

▶ **Front Line:** The front line consists of employees who directly interact with customers and perform the core activities that deliver the organization's products or services. For example: the call center employees, guest services, nurses and doctors.

We like the simplicity of this three-tier framework, and it holds up well for the purposes of cultural acceptance regardless of the scale and diversity of an organizational footprint. That said, if for practical or political reasons additional and separate roles need to be incorporated, that is certainly possible.

Once you have these tiers identified, start to examine the relative disposition of these audiences to CX within the tiers. With this, you are starting to think about how, for example, there are different attitudes among leaders or front-line employees that the organization needs to consider and address. Some will understand and embrace CX while others may actively reject it. You need to know this.

Disposition

Disposition ties back to the idea of individual perspective. We all know an ever-shifting continuum of attitude toward CX always exists. Our model (see Figure 8.2) looks at the CX cultural disposition in aggregate across conviction and confidence. In regard to conviction, you can look at whether there is an understanding of CX and a belief that it matters to the organization. In regard to confidence, you can examine whether there is belief in the ability to successfully execute CX efforts given corporate conditions such as leadership actively championing CX success and ensuring teams have the right training, tools, and resources to deliver CX efforts. You can survey staff to get an understanding of these dynamics.

Combining the two, you now have a more sophisticated attitudinal segmentation that can help to inform and drive targeted cultural development efforts. You can start to think about segments and cohorts versus specific individuals, per se (for example, the skeptical leader, the frontline seeker, the operational doer). You can put in place very specific actions to engage, sustain, and move more of the organization from one segment to the next. Let's examine each quadrant in Figure 8.2.

- How well do we grasp the significance of CX to our organization's success? (Understanding)

- To what degree do we believe that enhancing CX can result in improved business outcomes for our organization and our customers? (Belief)

All segments exist...

Conviction
(in understanding and belief)

"Seekers" "Advocates"

"Skeptics" "Doers"

Confidence
(in advocacy and support)

- Do our leaders actively champion CX success? (Advocacy)
- Do we provide CX teams with the right training, tools, and resources to be successful? (Support)

Figure 8.2: CX Cultural Disposition Framework

Advocates (high conviction, high confidence)

Advocates are individuals who both deeply understand and believe in the importance of customer experience and feel highly confident in their ability to execute CX initiatives effectively. They are not only aware of the value CX brings to the organization but are also assured that they have the leadership support, resources, and incentives necessary to drive CX efforts successfully.

Characteristics:

▶ Passionate about CX and its impact on business success
▶ Often take initiative and lead CX projects
▶ Serve as role models and mentors for others within the organization
▶ Actively seek out and implement best practices in CX

Example—The Advocate Leader—A C-suite executive who regularly champions CX strategies in leadership meetings; they give voice and air cover to the practice. They reward and recognize experience wins and encourage their operational staff to further embrace customer-centric practices. These are the individuals who serve as executive sponsors for big enterprise experience plays because they know they will make a difference.

Seekers (high conviction, low confidence)

Seekers are those who understand and believe in the importance of CX but lack confidence in their ability to successfully implement CX initiatives due to perceived or real constraints such as inadequate leadership support, insufficient resources, or misaligned incentives.

Characteristics:

- Strong belief in the value of CX but hesitant to take action due to lack of confidence
- Desire to improve CX but feel constrained by organizational barriers
- Seek opportunities for learning and support to build their confidence
- May become frustrated if not given the necessary tools and support

Example—The Operational Seeker—A middle manager who is passionate about enhancing customer experience but feels limited by a lack of budget and insufficient backing from upper management. They actively look for training and mentorship opportunities to overcome these barriers.

Doers (low conviction, high confidence)

Doers are confident in their ability to execute tasks and drive projects, but they lack a deep understanding or belief in the strategic importance of CX. They are effective at implementing initiatives but may not see the broader value of customer experience to the organization.

Characteristics:

- Highly skilled and capable of executing projects effectively
- Focus on task completion and operational efficiency
- May not prioritize CX unless explicitly directed to do so
- Require education on the strategic importance of CX to fully align their efforts

Example—The Operational Doer—A project manager who is excellent at meeting deadlines and managing resources but does not inherently prioritize customer feedback or consider the long-term impact of their projects on customer satisfaction.

Skeptics (low conviction, low confidence)

Skeptics neither believe strongly in the importance of CX nor feel confident in their ability to implement CX initiatives. They may be resistant to change and doubtful about the value of investing time and resources into customer experience efforts.

Characteristics:

▸ Skeptical about the benefits of CX and its impact on business success
▸ Lack confidence in their own or the organization's ability to execute CX initiatives
▸ May resist CX initiatives or see them as nonessential
▸ Require significant persuasion and evidence to change their mindset

Example—The Frontline Skeptic—A frontline employee who is disengaged and skeptical about new CX training programs, feeling that their daily tasks are more about process than customer impact. They tend to comply as directed but are not proactive in their interest to create positive customer experiences.

THE ROLE OF THE CEO

When we conducted a recent private study among health care CX Champions, they spoke extensively about how CEOs needed to support a culture of customer. We've included their responses here, using their own words. One sums up CEO involvement as, "I think we've had the positive support of a CEO who thought it was the be-all and end-all. Everything has the potential to go well if your leadership cares. So he really brought voice to that."

But CEOs change, and with that comes a potential rebalancing of strategic priorities. CX Champions are constantly managing up to engage, to channel, and create necessary CEO advocacy for efforts across the culture. In their minds, how would CEOs help?

Admit it.

CEO leaders in health care, who are often physicians, do not come from a culture of customer experience. It is something they learn to understand, to value (or not), and their receptivity to it will vary. "The good news is we've got to a healing of admission. No one on our executive team has background. Additionally, experience simply isn't something that's fully understood, and therefore, there is often resistance among system leaders. But it's also a fear thing." CEOs themselves need to acknowledge and model their own lack of understanding and their desire to learn alongside their system leadership teams.

Integrate it.

Experience work needs to be strategically intentional and accountable. CEO leaders must ensure not only that efforts are explicit within organizational strategic plans but that success is tied to executive compensation structures. "I wanted to make sure that, from the very top of the leadership, they really believe that the work that we do needs to be customer-centered. And I think when you go into an organization that believes that and rewards it and puts it in their strategic plan, your likelihood of success is so much greater."

Evangelize it.

As the top communicator, CX Champions want to see their CEOs embrace and imbue experience throughout their internal and external communications. "That's really critical. The language needs to start from the top and just permeate everything we do." It's the sense of personal ownership that "the CEO is speaking to the fact that we care for people, and that's it, right? That the buck stops there is incredibly important."

Celebrate it.

Leaders want their CEOs to shine the light and celebrate customer experience successes. Adding the personal attention and recognition is invaluable to the culture. "It was medicine for my soul to see these words and to be recognized—to be validated by our leader's appreciation."

Give it time.

"My motto has been to keep it simple and stay the course." Experience work is "a marathon." CEOs and their leadership teams need to have the right initial expectations around experience work and ensure that they appropriately nurture those efforts. Creating the necessary cultural conditions for long-term adoption for experience is "not an easy needle to move quickly."

Guide it.

All leaders acknowledge that experience work is messy. Meaningful efforts require new organizational collaborations, shared ownership, and blurred lines of responsibility. Much of the strategic intentionality for experience isn't set at the top; it's set by the leader practitioners. "So you got a bunch of us sitting around either going, 'Cool, we can start running' or 'This doesn't feel right. If I do something, am I gonna get creamed?'" These collaborations require a steady, visionary CEO leader that can encourage success through the ambiguity. They have an active hand in facilitating the right organizational decision and direction for experience efforts.

Intentionally Cultivate New CX Dispositions

CX work can't be off the side of the desk. It can't be "all of our responsibility" to nurture the culture. Yes, everyone can and should support CX, but their perspectives will be different and their explicit, ongoing involvement in CX efforts needs to be clear. It can't be shadow work that hopefully happens in the course of day-to-day activities. There's a perception that culture work is soft and it's more difficult to measure the outcome. It gets occasional attention and action through side doors of other initiatives (e.g., "let's do an award"). Simply put, it doesn't get the intentionality of other business activities. And we think that is a huge missed opportunity.

Culture work can and should be explicitly planned and actioned as rigorously as any other effort. There are direct linkages and accountabilities of positive cultural conditions to successful business outcomes for CX.

In our work, as detailed previously, we leverage an understanding of organizational disposition and existing cultural ingredients or drivers to inform a robust plan that can be actioned and measured by the CX leader. This hinges on a simple but extremely valuable framework to guide the right mix of cultural engagement activities. Look at each segment of the organization and essentially put an approach in place to engage and amplify their involvement in CX, as seen in the following Audience Engagement Model (Figure 8.3).

With this audience engagement model in place, CX Champions can evaluate and prioritize segment activities based on their CX strategies. In what ways does the organizational culture footprint need to change to achieve the stated goals of the CX strategy? And, conversely, in which ways will realization of the CX strategy change cultural attitudes? This kind of strategic alignment can set in motion the exciting and more familiar work to plan appropriate tactical activities to achieve segment-specific plans (e.g., executive roadshows, customer storytelling, rewards and recognition programs). These individual efforts can now be laddered back through to direct goals and the vision of the CX strategy itself.

Let's look at the example of insight workshops addressed in chapter 4, "Insights." Here, we address a robust, deep understanding of customers' rational and emotional needs and expectations as an essential component of permanent CX

	"ADVOCATES"	"DOERS"	"SEEKERS"	"SKEPTICS"
Overall approach	Champion and mobilize	Engage and enlighten	Support and develop	Inform and inspire
	Leverage their strong belief and confidence in CX by empowering them to lead initiatives, mentor others, and build a customer-centric culture throughout the organization.	Educate them on the strategic value of CX and align their efforts with broader CX objectives, leveraging their operational efficiency to enhance customer experience.	Build their confidence through targeted support, training, and mentorship, enabling them to effectively translate their conviction in CX into actionable and successful efforts.	Gradually introduce to the importance of CX through educational sessions and involvement in CX activities, aiming to shift their perspective and build their belief and confidence.
For leadership, this means	Empower and leverage their influence to drive CX culture.	Educate and align their efforts with the strategic importance of CX.	Build their confidence through support and structured development.	Persuade with evidence and provide robust support structures.
For operators, this means	Utilize their operational expertise to implement and optimize CX initiatives.	Link their operational efficiency to CX outcomes.	Provide tools and training to boost their confidence in CX execution.	Educate and involve them in small-scale CX initiatives to build understanding and trust.
For the front line, this means	Engage them as front-line champions who exemplify and promote CX excellence.	Connect their daily tasks with the broader CX objectives.	Encourage and support their development through hands-on experience and mentorship.	Engage them in practical hands-on activities that demonstrate the value of CX.

Figure 8.3: Audience Engagement Model

at scale. We all know that simply conducting research and learning about customers is only the first step in the process of empathy at scale. Organizations need to onboard these insights, show how they can be leveraged, and envision how experiences might change based on these insights. Further, this must be reinforced over time, versioned by segment in the audience engagement model. At one global software vendor, we developed a program of tactics to deliver these mandates, consisting of intranet tools, physical artifacts distributed to execution teams, integrating in planning and execution processes empathy insights, training modules for all new hires into CX execution teams, and a range of other tactics to create a portfolio approach to connecting doers and seekers.

Creating a successful CX culture means tapping into the strengths and values that are already part of the organization. It's not about changing but rather reconnecting with what makes the company great. By focusing on advocates, seekers, doers, and skeptics, the experience leader can tailor efforts to boost confidence and understanding where it's needed most. Don't leave it to chance or hope that it's a natural outcome of other CX efforts. Give it targeted support, oversight, and clear alignment to goals.

BEFORE & AFTER

Before Culture: Operational Focus

A global technology client had drifted from a company built on customer intimacy to one based on financials, cost cutting, and next quarter's earnings. It became focused on sales at all costs, resulting in customers being sold products they didn't need, sales processes that felt aggressive and forced, and a damaged reputation for a once-lauded brand. In meetings, the customer was discussed only as an asset to be leveraged, not as a person to be served well. They needed a return to the customer as true north to turn around customer sentiment—to once again naturally attract customers instead of having to pull them in.

After Culture: Customer Focus

When a new CEO took control of the organization, they mandated that the customer would become the focal point. It wasn't just a public declaration; it was about using the levers of leadership to steer the underlying culture. The CEO aligned strategies and leadership incentives to CX performance, established internal awards, and highlighted customer conversations. They channeled the voice of both customers and employees, investing time and resources to listen and engage. By sponsoring key enterprise-wide customer efforts to jump start CX, the new CEO became the model of commitment the organization needed. This hands-on leadership, combined with other CX development efforts, led to a 20 percent increase in employee understanding and confidence in CX, as reflected in engagement surveys.

Key Points Recap

- CX should amplify and reconnect with existing positive cultural attributes rather than attempting to change the company's culture.
- An organization's culture will always encompass diverse attitudes toward CX, requiring tailored strategies for different groups.
- Nurturing a positive CX culture demands real, intentional work, deeply integrating CX principles into the organization.
- Successful CX culture relies on strong leadership and broad employee engagement, ensuring everyone knows their role in enhancing customer experience.

We've taken you through the five critical enablers of Strategic CX at scale: insights, CX strategy, blueprints, operating model, and culture. Now what?

CONCLUSION

Moving Forward and Taking Action

CX is together work. Together we—you in your company, all of us in the CX community—can all do something exciting that drives change in businesses individually and in business generally.

If you are seeking to advance in your current position, to learn by doing, to create meaning in your work, or to do something different to reawaken your *why*, take something from this book and apply it in your role.

Find a CX collaborator within your organization, set up a meeting, and review the CX assessment in chapter 3 to get the juices flowing. Find an entry point to get started, whether that's a broader meeting with colleagues, a decision to do some customer research, or identifying an initiative you can influence that incorporates the customer more intentionally.

More importantly: identify as a CX Champion. Make it part of your identity, of who you are as a player on the field of business. Say, "I am a CX Champion," as opposed to, "I work in CX."

As CX Practitioners, we have the power to impact other people's lives at scale. What a worthy pursuit—to put some good into the world, into our markets, into our companies. We have the power to correct the Great Distancing, to begin a pivot toward customer centricity.

Remember the critical components of CX at scale:

- **Empathy insights** to fuel CX efforts. Remember to include emotions customers feel across the end-to-end customer experience. Get to know customers as humans. Picture them in your mind's eye. Think about them and obsess over their needs and expectations.

- **Strategy** to coordinate and align efforts. Point everyone in the same direction by thinking critically about the experience you ultimately want to create, then make that simple and clear so team members get it instantly.

- **Blueprints** to be precise, intentional, and thoughtful about the experiences you want to create for customers. From the ordinary experiences to the special touches, thinking through the details of the experience is where the work of experience starts to become tangible.

- **Operating model** to ensure organizational adoption of CX practices and to formalize the pursuit of CX at scale. Build the internal relationships and shared purpose necessary to sustain CX success.

- **Culture** to ensure that you increase team members' belief in CX. Help everyone in your organization recognize its criticality and impact. You are bumping up against decades of ingrained beliefs that have resulted in the Great Distancing. There is much work to be done, but we have found that teams are eager to consider change when presented with the benefits of customer centricity.

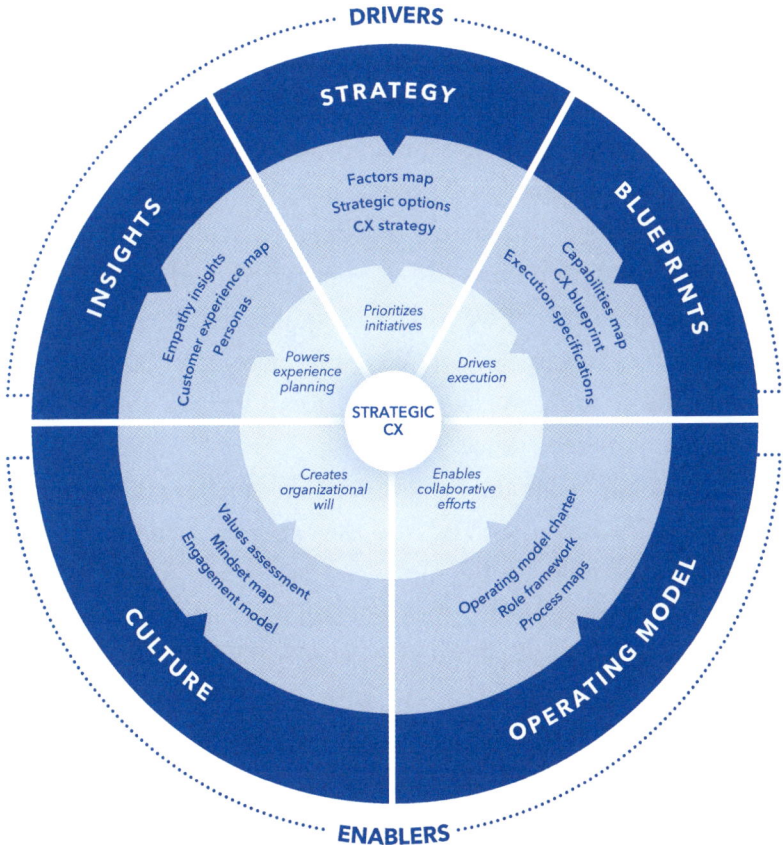

Think about these components and how each plate needs to be spinning (eventually) to achieve high-performance CX. But don't let what may feel like massive gaps lock you or your company up. It may seem daunting to go from the current state to a desired future state. CX Champions and CX Practitioners need to break down this gap into smaller, achievable wins. We all need to feel the joy of small wins, gaining a foothold, and creating momentum.

Your organization will be on its own journey, navigating its own path to success. Along this path, the organization will face various twists and turns, experimenting, succeeding, and sometimes failing with CX. Ideally, it will mature in its deliberate adoption of CX as a fundamental practice for driving success. The company will become part of the CX revolution, refocusing its efforts on the customer to achieve its goals. This book outlined the five core practices and numerous detailed models that we believe can guide the enterprise on this journey toward success. We want the company's journey to be successful, and we believe it can be. We've seen it happen numerous times.

CX Champions and Practitioners like you have the power to make it happen. You possess the expertise, acumen, and intention to help your company be better at CX. You will have made it happen because you will have applied some of the practices and models we've shared.

We hope this book has been of service. We encourage you to share your expertise with us and others. Together, let's all be part of the revolution that is so vital for the future of business.

ACKNOWLEDGMENTS

To all the clients and teams we've had the privilege of working with since founding WideOpen and even before—thank you. While we've worked hard to help you solve challenges, the truth is, we've learned just as much from you. Your experiences, insights, and collaboration have shaped the way we think and work.

We also want to extend our heartfelt thanks to some key individuals who have been unwavering supporters, collaborators, and advocates for what we do. Lin MacMaster, Nicole Elsner, and Götz Bockstedte, your partnerships have been invaluable. We couldn't have come this far without your dedication and belief in the power of CX.

To the incredible team at WideOpen—dozens of bright, energetic, and passionate experts who have been a part of this journey—thank you. In particular, Debby Chow, who has been a trusted collaborator over the years, and Michael Epple, our go-to research guru. You've both been instrumental in the work we've done.

And finally, to our friends, parents, and families—Jodi, Shauna, Tyler, Charlotte, Maya, and Jack—your encouragement and support made all the difference. You've stood by us, and you're the reason we've been able to thrive.

ABOUT THE AUTHORS

Mark Fithian and **Jeff Rosenberg** are the cofounders of WideOpen, a Strategic CX consulting company.

Mark's customer strategy expertise and methodologies were developed through over thirty years of work across multiple industries, collaborating with leading brands such as Providence, SAP, PayPal, Optum, IBM, BMW, the American Cancer Society, and Microsoft. Before cofounding WideOpen, Mark held key roles in both client-side and agency-side positions, as well as in strategic consultancies.

Jeff has spent more than thirty years working across strategy, operations, and customer experience disciplines, consulting for leading companies such as SAP, Verizon, Hershey, Optum, BMW, ADT, and Motorola. Prior to cofounding WideOpen, Jeff served in leadership and practitioner roles in consulting, agency, and corporate organizations.